BAUDELAIRE AND *LE SPLEEN DE PARIS*

. . . mes élucubrations en prose.
Baudelaire

Baudelaire and
Le Spleen de Paris

J. A. HIDDLESTON

CLARENDON PRESS · OXFORD
1987

Oxford University Press, Walton Street, Oxford, OX2 6DP
Oxford New York Toronto
Delhi Bombay Calcutta Madras Karachi
Petaling Jaya Singapore Hong Kong Tokyo
Nairobi Dar es Salaam Cape Town
Melbourne Auckland
and associated companies in
Beirut Berlin Ibadan Nicosia

Oxford is a trade mark of Oxford University Press

Published in the United States
by Oxford University Press, New York

British Library Cataloguing in Publication Data
Data available

Library of Congress Cataloging in Publication Data
Hiddleston, J. A. (James Andrew)
Baudelaire and Le spleen de Paris.
Bibliography: p.
Includes index.
1. Baudelaire, Charles, 1821–1867. Spleen de Paris.
I. Title.
PQ2191.S63H5   1986   841'.8   86-21682
ISBN 0-19-815839-4
ISBN 0-19-815845-9 (pbk.)

Phototypeset by Dobbie Typesetting Service, Plymouth, Devon
Printed in Great Britain
at the University Printing House, Oxford
by David Stanford
Printer to the University

Preface

Uncertainty surrounds all aspects of Baudelaire's prose poems. What he wished to, and what he did, achieve in experimenting with such a 'dangerous' and hybrid genre, in which he had few predecessors, none of whom have been incorporated in the literary canon, is by no means evident; we do not know what the completed volume would have looked like or even how many pieces it would have contained, and there has been disagreement about the title he would have chosen. Furthermore, the reader may well feel deprived of guides and norms; for, in contrast with the voluminous bibliography of *Les Fleurs du Mal*, very little has appeared on the prose poems. Fritz Nies's *Poesie in prosaischer Welt*, the only full-length study, came out more than twenty years ago, and although there has been a considerable increase in publication in recent years particularly in the form of articles, many of which make a distinguished contribution to an aspect of the subject, Barbara Johnson's *Défigurations du langage poétique* is the only major work to have appeared since. Dedicated to Paul de Man, it contains many illuminating insights, but its often highly ingenious arguments are based almost exclusively on the doublets of 1857 and 'Le Galant Tireur', with the result that the view of the poems that emerges is inevitably incomplete. By examining the position of the artist and his attitude towards his art, the complex and often ambiguous moral message the poems suggest, and above all the relationship between prose and poetry, I have tried to dispel some of the obscurities which envelop the texts. I have used throughout the title *Le Spleen de Paris*, since, whatever his hesitations, it is the one Baudelaire uses increasingly in his correspondence after 1863 and, given his predilection for titles which are either 'pétards' or 'mystérieux', seems much preferable to *Petits Poëmes en prose*, which serves merely to designate a genre.

I am deeply grateful to the British Academy for a grant which enabled me to visit the 'Centre d'Études baudelairiennes' at Vanderbilt

University, to the editors of *Nineteenth-Century French Studies*, *Bulletin baudelairien*, and *Modern Language Review* for permission to use material which I had published in these journals, and especially to Professor Claude Pichois for reading the manuscript and for much friendly help and wise counsel.

J. A. Hiddleston

Exeter College, Oxford
1986

Contents

I

Art and the Artist

Whatever Baudelaire's hesitations about what he wished to achieve in the prose poems, and whatever the increasing creative difficulties he encountered—'Ah! ce *Spleen*, quelles colères, et quel labeur il m'a causés!'[1]—it emerges from the many references to them in his correspondence that he thought of them as complementing *Les Fleurs du Mal* and providing a kind of companion volume.

In December 1862 he talks of the two works as 'se faisant pendant réciproquement',[2] and as late as 1866 he writes of the prose poems as being 'encore *Les Fleurs du Mal*, mais avec beaucoup plus de liberté, et de détail, et de raillerie'.[3] In order to give expression to all the bitterness and bad humour of which he says he is full,[4] he constantly places the emphasis upon an intensification of that clash of opposites—Spleen and Ideal, God and Satan, 'extase de la vie' and 'horreur de la vie'[5]—which is, of course, among the most striking and powerful characteristics of *Les Fleurs du Mal*. To this end, he says, he will associate 'l'effrayant avec le bouffon, et même la tendresse avec la haine'.[6] But, although there are very obvious similarities of theme and emotional preoccupation which the reader might expect from works stemming from the same temperament and belonging to the same poetic universe, the differences between the two volumes are many and profound; for Baudelaire is not just experimenting with a new poetic technique and form, not just intensifying the ironic stridency and disharmony caused by the clash of disparate and incongruous emotions and experiences, he also appears, in spite of his fears of producing a mere 'plaquette'[7] or slim volume of random musings, to have come to a new conception of what might constitute a volume of poetry.

In order to sense what Barbey d'Aurevilly called its secret architecture,[8] the reader need not accept the views of those who would see in *Les Fleurs du Mal* a kind of tragedy in which the tragic hero comes to grief,[9] or of those who would invite us to read the work

1

as if it had something resembling the structure and plot of a novel. It may well have been the poet himself who alerted Barbey to this perhaps too well concealed architecture, and who encouraged him to write the famous essay in an attempt to show that his claim at the trial of 1857, where *Les Fleurs du Mal* was alleged to be immoral and blasphemous, that the work had a moral message, was not just special pleading, but a truth evident to the most distinguished experts. At the time of the publication of the second edition in which he was at pains to strengthen and emphasize this sense of an architecture, Baudelaire writes to Vigny in a letter of December 1861:[10]

Le seul éloge que je sollicite pour ce livre est qu'on reconnaisse qu'il n'est pas un pur album et qu'il a un commencement et une fin. Tous les poèmes nouveaux ont été faits pour être adaptés au cadre singulier que j'avais choisi.

In a word, the meaning and the 'morality' Baudelaire wishes increasingly to see in the work are inherent in its structure, and the role of art is to record a spiritual journey, indicating a progressive disillusionment with the here and now and with the senses after a frantic immersion in them. Unlike the first edition which concentrates on the figure of the poet,[11] the second shows the spiritual dilemma of modern man, a prey to the tyranny of modern civilization, and more particularly of his own irremediably fallen nature. Because of its universality (Baudelaire speaks as the bad conscience of all men as his address to the 'Hypocrite lecteur, — mon semblable, — mon frère!' indicates), and because of its comprehensive view of the passions and human nature, *Les Fleurs du Mal* presents a kind of synthesis of experience, both physical and spiritual, from the standpoint of an austere, unorthodox, vacillating, and restricted Christianity. In spite of his claim that 'le livre partait d'une idée catholique',[12] by which he clearly means the idea of original sin, there is no sense of a redemption through Christ, who in 'Le Reniement de saint Pierre' is presented as a failure. Although Baudelaire is at pains elsewhere to point to the simultaneous pull of the contradictory elements in man,[13] and although the poems were clearly not written in the order in which they appear in the collection, by arranging them in that order, and by strengthening the original cadre, he has given the impression of a development and of a synthesis of experience.

In a recent book Leo Bersani has cast some doubt on the validity of the idea of the 'architecture' of *Les Fleurs du Mal*, since 'what

is begun and what is ended is an experiment that might have resulted
in a universe of meaning in which beginnings and endings would
be irrelevant'.[14] There is clearly much merit in such a view which
stresses the relative and contingent aspects of Baudelaire's outlook
and poetic experience. It remains that in *Les Fleurs du Mal*, and in
particular in the second edition, the poet has made an act of faith
in the power of the intellect to bring order into, and synthesize
the anarchy of, experience from birth to death. Professor Bersani
also suggests that the famous simultaneous postulations towards
God and Satan can in fact be thought of as a means of escape from
the Baudelairean discovery of what he calls 'psychic mobility' and
'unanchored identity'.[15] It is indeed true that these postulations, and
the whole system of binary opposites which structure his world-view,
enable the poet to define himself, providing a sense of identity in
a world whose poles at least are fixed; whoever and whatever he
is, he exists in relation to these stable truths. To illustrate the point,
one need only contrast Baudelaire with, say, the decadent Laforgue
who has no sense of original sin or of moral conflict, and whose
various personae suffer from a feeling of indeterminacy in both the
inner and the outer worlds, where 'le semblable, c'est le contraire';[16]
whereas with Baudelaire, whose world sometimes degenerates into
a nightmare, the notion of original sin is a permanent, immutable
truth which, in spite of everything, situates him in the moral and
physical universe. But to be fully convincing Bersani would have to
show either that Baudelaire had somehow discarded the Christian-
Platonist conception of the relationship of mind to body which
informs his writings, or that such a conception was merely a sham
of bad faith and did not consequently form in reality the basis of
his view of the world.[17]

However that may be, when we turn from *Les Fleurs du Mal* to
Le Spleen de Paris, we find no such effort towards unity or a scheme
of things. We pass from an attempt at synthesis to fragmentation,
contradiction, and uncertainty. In this respect the prose poems appear
more disillusioned and pessimistic, since what remains after our
reading of the fifty pieces is an impression of perpetual clash and
of sentimental and moral anarchy. Fragmentation, discontinuity,
external and internal chaos are the essential elements of this work,
itself only a fragment, which is meant to depict the disharmony of
modern man both by its content and by its form. Baudelaire's claim
to Vigny in 1861 that *Les Fleurs du Mal* is not a mere album of

poems, but that it has a beginning and an end, contrasts sharply with the 'dédicace' to Arsène Houssaye for the twenty prose poems published in *La Presse* in August and September 1862, when he permits the director of the review to publish the poems in any order and to omit whichever ones he pleases:

Mon cher ami, je vous envoie un petit ouvrage dont on ne pourrait pas dire, sans injustice, qu'il n'a ni queue ni tête, puisque tout, au contraire, y est à la fois tête et queue, alternativement et réciproquement. Considérez, je vous prie, quelles admirables commodités cette combinaison nous offre à tous, à vous, à moi et au lecteur. Nous pouvons couper où nous voulons, moi ma rêverie, vous le manuscrit, le lecteur sa lecture; car je ne suspends pas la volonté rétive de celui-ci au fil interminable d'une intrigue superflue.[18]

There being no 'plot', the dislocation of the 'petit ouvrage' would appear to be intentional, and there is no attempt to group the poems according to theme or 'genre', or to give the impression of a development or intensification. 'Le Mauvais Vitrier' is placed far from 'Assommons les pauvres!', as are 'Le Fou et la Vénus' from 'Le Vieux Saltimbanque', and 'Les Yeux des pauvres' from 'Le Joujou du pauvre', in spite of the obvious thematic similarities. Nor is there any evidence of an attempt to proceed by antithesis, whether of individual poems ('Les Foules' is not juxtaposed to 'La Solitude', nor is 'Le Chien et le flacon' to 'Les Bons Chiens') or of groups of poems. Of course, we have no clear idea how Baudelaire would have arranged the collection if he had completed it, bringing the number of poems possibly up to one hundred, the same as in the first edition of *Les Fleurs du Mal*.[19] The divisions—'Choses parisiennes', 'Onéirocritie', 'Symboles et moralités'—which can be found in the 'Listes de projets'[20] may correspond to those which he intended for the completed collection or they may simply have been for his own guidance. But as late as January 1866, when all but eight of the prose poems had been published, his intention still appears to be to produce a work in which the order would be random, as a letter to Sainte-Beuve indicates:[21] 'j'ai l'espoir de pouvoir montrer, un de ces jours, un nouveau Joseph Delorme accrochant sa pensée *rapsodique* à chaque accident de sa flânerie . . .'. In 'Le Poème du hachisch' he defines rhapsodic as 'un train de pensées suggéré et commandé par le monde extérieur et le hasard des circonstances',[22] and quotes the passage in Poe where 'le nerveux Auguste Bedloe' claims that, after his morning dose of opium, the outside world has become much more intensely interesting, the merest objects creating 'tout un monde d'inspirations, une procession magnifique et bigarrée de pensées désordonnées et rhapsodiques'.[23] The collection as we have it, and probably also as it was conceived, would then appear to provide an excellent example of one aspect of the decadent style as defined by Bourget in his brilliant study on Baudelaire in *Essais de psychologie contemporaine*: 'celui où l'unité du livre se décompose pour laisser la place à l'indépendance de la page . . . ';[24] and *Le Spleen de Paris* with its uncertain, hybrid, and varied genre and its emphasis on fragmentation and uncertainty shows some of the formal characteristics of such masterpieces of decadent literature as *La Tentation de saint Antoine*, *A rebours*, and *Les Nourritures terrestres*. There is no sense of a development or of an unfolding, the sudden changes in tone and theme conform to no pattern, and the poet appears buffeted from one mood to another in a world which seems devoid of any transcendence or hope of transcendence, or of any synthesizing factor. Although the devil in 'Le Joueur généreux' appears, in spite of the theological seriousness of his utterances, as a caricature, the 'idée catholique' of original sin is all the stronger for the absence of lasting positive values and the absence of any possibility of grace through God or through art. The postulation towards Satan and evil remains a reality whereas the postulation towards God or the ideal is an illusion, as is the belief in the synthesizing power of the intellect. Furthermore, in these prose pieces, which are clearly linked to his *Journaux intimes* and have a considerable confessional quality, Baudelaire seems less bent upon talking for all mankind and upon establishing universal truths about modern life in general, than upon recording the accidental commotions 'd'*une* vie moderne'.[25]

In the prose poems there is no unequivocal eulogy of the artist whose position and function appear, to say the least, problematic. 'L'Étranger', one of the most enduringly popular pieces, is significant in this respect. The artist is of course an outcast, as in *Les Fleurs du Mal*, without family and friends and homeland. His only escape is in the contemplation of clouds: he is the ineffectual dreamer whose dreams are as pliable and as insubstantial as the clouds themselves. His reverie is pure escapism as in 'La Soupe et les nuages'; he does not even have the innocence and faith of the child in 'Les Vocations' who sees God 'assis sur ce petit nuage isolé, ce petit nuage couleur de feu, qui marche doucement'; for the child's naïve reverie is coupled with a religious exaltation, which in the adult outsider degenerates

into escapism. Also, the contrast with 'Élévation' is striking, where
the rising of the mind is accompanied by an aspiration towards God
or a higher order of things:

> Au-dessus des étangs, au-dessus des vallées,
> Des montagnes, des bois, des nuages, des mers,
> Par-delà le soleil, par-delà les éthers,
> Par-delà les confins des sphères étoilées,
> Mon esprit, tu te meus avec agilité [. . .]

The clouds in 'L'Étranger' denote mobility, change, and the ability
to go anywhere out of this world, horizontally. There is nothing of
the powerful verticality of 'Élévation' whose dynamism, virility, and
energy contrast with the relaxed and passive musing of the 'étranger'.
   In this first piece the position of the artist and the nature of his
art are, thus, already problematical: firstly, because the clouds with
their floating, horizontal movement present no transcendence; and
secondly, because the poet's declaration that he hates gold as much
as other men hate God does not imply a positive belief on his part,
a belief which is all the more painfully absent for having been evoked
by the discreet biblical intertext in Luke 14: 26: 'If any man come
to me, and hate not his father, and mother, and wife, and children,
and brethren, and sisters, yea, and his own life also, he cannot be
my disciple.' Commenting on the 'merveilleux nuages' 'qui sont
comme un symbole de son surnaturalisme', Robert Kopp compares
'L'Étranger' and a passage in the 1859 *Salon* where Baudelaire praises
the splendid skyscapes of the painter Boudin.[26] But the conditions
are entirely different. Here Baudelaire is talking of the depiction of
clouds, stressing, in a passage which was to delight Gaston Bachelard
in *L'Air et les songes*,[27] their colour, richness, variety, their 'formes
fantastiques', 'ténèbres chaotiques', 'immensités vertes'. He describes
how the clouds seem to appeal to the imagination to fashion shapes
and how they have the power to enchant the mind like an opium
dream, whereas in 'L'Étranger' the emphasis is on the transient nature
of 'les nuages qui passent'. Likewise, Lemaître quotes a passage[28]
from the 1846 *Salon* about Delacroix: 'les nuages, délayés et tirés
en sens divers comme une gaze qui se déchire, sont d'une grande
légèreté; et cette voûte d'azur, profonde et lumineuse, fuit à une
prodigieuse hauteur.' But here again, a thematic approach must be
attentive to the context, and one should avoid the error of thinking
that clouds have only one value or meaning within the poet's mental

universe. Clearly, what excites Baudelaire in Delacroix's clouds is not their transitory nature, but the way they appear to increase the depth of the azure blue sky above them. They at once veil the infinite and exaggerate it by their transparency and by the rents in them. They thus correspond to a fundamental requirement in Baudelaire's aesthetic of 'le fini dans l'infini' which he spells out in the 1859 *Salon*,[29] in his appreciation of a painting called 'Petites Mouettes', which he describes as depicting 'l'azur intense du ciel et de l'eau, deux quartiers de roche qui font une porte ouverte sur l'infini', adding significantly in parenthesis 'vous savez que l'infini paraît plus profond quand il est plus resserré'. The contrast with 'L'Étranger', where there is no suggestion of the infinite or of a transcendence, could not therefore be clearer.

However, a parallel might more properly be said to exist between 'L'Étranger' and 'Le Port'; for a port, like clouds, is a 'séjour charmant pour une âme fatiguée des luttes de la vie'. The 'étranger''s contemplation of clouds is accompanied by a dismissal of everything terrestrial and mundane. Similarly, in the port the poet scorns the agitation of those base souls who have still 'la force de vouloir, le désir de voyager ou de s'enrichir'. There is in the two poems the same languid detachment, the same disenchanted 'vague-à-l'âme', and the same relaxed fascination with the endless variety of clouds and sea which ceaselessly and pointlessly amuse the eye and the minds of those who have no more curiosity or ambition: 'l'ampleur du ciel, l'architecture mobile des nuages, les colorations changeantes de la mer, le scintillement des phares, sont un prisme merveilleusement propre à amuser les yeux sans jamais les lasser.' The same parallel is brought out in 'Les Bienfaits de la lune' where those who have been affected by the kiss of the moon will be forced for ever to love those things connected with it, 'l'eau, les nuages, le silence et la nuit; la mer immense et verte; l'eau informe et multiforme; le lieu où tu ne seras pas; l'amant que tu ne connaîtras pas'. Sea and clouds are, then, united in Baudelaire's imagination in these prose poems as the ideal country of those who have lived out the truth that action is not 'la sœur du rêve',[30] and who have given themselves over, devoid of will or ambition, to the fruitless contemplation of ever-changing chimera.[31]

The position of the artist and the nature of art are problematical also because of the 'étranger''s enigmatic reply when asked if he loves beauty above all else; 'Je l'aimerais volontiers, déesse et immortelle.'

The implication of the conditional is clear; he would love beauty if it could be created or attained in some manner, or if it were in any sense rewarding; but since this is not the case, the contemplation of clouds and the accompanying mental relaxation provide escape and consolation. The poem is clearly linked to number XVII of *Les Fleurs du Mal* where beauty is seen as divine and immortal; but, although in 'La Beauté' the poet undergoes great suffering, he is recompensed in his austere cult and adoration by the 'purs miroirs qui font toutes choses plus belles'. The implication of the poet's lethargy in 'L'Étranger' is his disbelief in any realizable form of beauty, an implication which is spelled out in 'Le *Confiteor* de l'artiste' where he exclaims in exasperation and despair that 'l'étude du beau est un duel où l'artiste crie de frayeur avant d'être vaincu'.

In *Les Fleurs du Mal* the artist enjoys considerable prestige, particularly in the poems which appear early in the collection. Although rejected like the 'étranger' by mother, father, and the rest of society, he has some compensations. In 'Bénédiction' he keeps his innocence, 'Il joue avec le vent, cause avec le nuage', and there is the promise of salvation through suffering:

> Je sais que vous gardez une place au Poète
> Dans les rangs bienheureux des saintes Légions,
> Et que vous l'invitez à l'éternelle fête
> Des Trônes, des Vertus, des Dominations.

In 'L'Albatros', although when exiled on earth the poet is a figure of fun and derision whose 'ailes de géant l'empêchent de marcher', the compensation is that he is a 'prince des nuées / Qui hante la tempête et se rit de l'archer'. Of course, the presentation of the artist is far from being uniformly optimistic. Several poems such as 'La Muse vénale' and 'La Mort des artistes' show him in a much more sombre light, and the struggle with his public or with the Angel of beauty is unevenly pitched against him. But these poems which show the defeat or distress of the artist, are balanced by others like 'Les Phares' which celebrate his triumph, and they are part of the general dialectic of good and evil, positive and negative, which gives structure to the collection, whose aim is to show both his grandeur and his 'misère'.

In *Le Spleen de Paris*, however, there is no such compensation or counterbalance. In 'Le Chien et le flacon' the poet is totally misunderstood by his readers, who would prefer the literary equivalent of the excrement which he should have offered his dog in place of the exquisite scent he had bought from the best perfumer in the town. 'La Corde'[32] presents an even more disquieting view of the artist and a much more subtly ambivalent one also. On the surface, the story is an ironic comment on the illusory nature of maternal love; it is supposedly a 'fait vrai' taken from the life of Manet and from which Baudelaire wishes to extract an unpleasant moral message. But a closer look reveals that it also has something, very discreetly, to say about the role of art and of the artist. Manet is supposed in this little 'conte cruel' to be relating how he found in his part of Paris a little boy whose 'physionomie ardente et espiègle' attracted him and whom, with the consent of his poor parents who were glad to be rid of him, he made into a little servant and model. His face, which is mobile and interesting, serves Manet well, who dresses him up in all sorts of guises: 'je l'ai transformé tantôt en petit bohémien, tantôt en ange, tantôt en Amour mythologique. Je lui ai fait porter le violon du vagabond, la Couronne d'Épines et les Clous de la Passion, et la Torche d'Éros', and no doubt he makes great pictures. Beyond his suitability as a model, what interests Manet in the boy is what he refers to as his 'drôlerie'. The boy takes to stealing Manet's sugar and liqueurs, is admonished by Manet who threatens to send him back to his parents, whereupon in despair the boy hangs himself. The rest of the story is given to a description of the dead boy and to the reactions of the mother who comes to ask the painter for the rope the boy hanged himself with, not in order to have 'une horrible et chère relique' of her son, but in order to sell pieces of it to superstitious people who think that 'la corde du pendu' brings good fortune. The moral lesson would seem then to be that even so fundamental an instinct as maternal love cannot be taken for granted.[33]

But there is surely in the first part of the poem an ironical comment on the nature of art which can convey through the model the attractions of Eros and the sufferings of Christ, but is unconscious of the real suffering which literally stands before it. The beauty of Eros and the passion of Christ are by implication mere games, amusements, totally devoid of seriousness, for all their power to persuade and move. Furthermore, we may ask if there is not some irresponsibility in Manet's attitude which is revealed in the light-hearted, flippant, and self-satisfied tone in which he talks glibly of his 'petit bonhomme', 'ma profession de peintre', and his special artistic faculty 'qui rend à nos yeux la vie plus vivante et plus significative que pour les autres hommes'. One might therefore be tempted to interpret the story as an attack on Manet to whom it was dedicated at the time of its publication in the *Figaro*[34] and as a confirmation of the poet's hesitations about his art. According to Philippe Rebeyrol and Lois Hyslop,[35] Baudelaire did not fully appreciate Manet, '*premier dans la décrépitude de votre art*',[36] because he did not paint from memory and consequently his pictures could not appeal to the memory of the spectator. His art, then, appeared to be limited to a superficial realism, devoid of those qualities— movement, aspiration towards the infinite, 'mnémotechnie'— which made the greatness of Delacroix, and which are essential for truly romantic art.[37]

But such an interpretation appears unjust and arbitrary, since Baudelaire is at pains to endow the painter in the poem with all kinds of qualities which belong to himself: in certain ways Manet resembles the 'rôdeur parisien', the disenchanted view of human nature is typically Baudelairean, and the various roles which the little boy is obliged to play do not correspond to any known paintings of Manet's, but are carefully chosen to represent, as in 'Les Vocations', fundamental aspects of Baudelaire's own temperament. It seems clear that he would not have drawn Manet to himself in this way with the sole aim of denouncing him as an artist. It seems equally clear that what is being called in question is not so much Manet's art, but the art of the poet himself, and that in 'La Corde' there is a kind of 'mise en abyme' through which the poem gives rise to the same problems, and is open to the same objections, as the fictional paintings it evokes. After all, the pictures never existed, and Manet is known to have used the boy as a model only in 'L'Enfant aux cerises' and 'Le Garçon et le chien'.[38] What does exist is Baudelaire's prose poem, composed and read one or two days only after the death of the boy in the presence of the painter and his friends. The real moral message would appear to be that art, whether the painter's or the poet's, is unable to come to grips with reality, which it avoids or fails to recognize. In the poem art is a lie replacing the living reality by a simulacrum, a comedy, which appeals only to the eye of the spectator or the reader without involving true emotions; so that the problematics of the piece involve not only the artist as creator, but also the reader who, if he is sensitive to poetry, enjoys a purely aesthetic thrill thanks to real suffering. The real torment of the boy has become an aesthetic experience in Baudelaire's poem just as much as in Manet's hypothetical paintings, so that it is possible to read 'La Corde' as a moral and aesthetic indictment of itself. Baudelaire seems here to be expressing his despair at what Proust, in a moment of literary agnosticism, called the 'magie illusoire de la littérature',[39] and to be asking the anguished question: What is the value of art if, in veiling the terrors of the abyss, it screens also from men's eyes the contemplation of real suffering?

Whether or not Baudelaire intended the poem to call itself in question, we can see that the figure of the artist has lost much of the prestige and 'gloire' which the Romantics claimed for him. In 'Perte d'auréole', which has its origins in the popular saying 'les auréoles changent souvent de tête', he has lost his halo and has fallen to the same level of spiritual mediocrity as other ordinary mortals. Following Jean Prévost, Robert Kopp is surely right to see the poem as 'une réplique désabusée'[40] to 'Bénédiction' in *Les Fleurs du Mal*; indeed the poem would be almost meaningless without a knowledge of its intertext and of the attendant mythology concerning the superiority of the artist and his salvation through his vision of the divine and through suffering. Having lost his halo while dodging the traffic in the busy streets of Paris, the poet has clearly lost any pretence to being considered some kind of sacred figure. As Richard Klein writes:

The Narrator demystifies all the Romantic pretensions implied by the halo, from within a world whose fictionality is constituted by the presence of the symbol he renounces. In short, he demystifies the symbol which in turn demystifies him.[41]

Klein also emphasizes the accidental loss of the halo which is contrasted with the poetic destiny which singles out the poet in 'Bénédiction'. Indeed, the poet is very much caught up in the contingencies of the material world which cause his halo to fall into the mud in the overcrowded and dangerous streets 'où la mort arrive au galop de tous les côtés à la fois'. An accident can make one lose one's poetic calling with perhaps the same suddenness as falling out of love or losing one's faith, or being knocked down by a carriage. But if it can be lost so easily, it can equally easily be restored or picked up out of the gutter by other people, and, with the detached curiosity of the dandy, the poet speculates on who among the mediocre poets of his circle might pick it up and wear it, and with what pleasant or unpleasant consequences. Unlike the 'beau diadème éblouissant et clair' of 'Bénédiction',[42] the halo is essentially valueless, an empty bauble, and its loss or finding are of little consequence, a mere accident or chance encounter. What was once sacred can be picked up in the streets and worn by charlatans.

In the prose poems the poet is principally identified with the mountebank, the fool, and the buffoon, as in 'Le Vieux Saltimbanque', 'Le Fou et la Vénus', and 'Une mort héroïque'. In *Les Fleurs du Mal* there are similar references; in 'La Muse vénale', where he is compared to a 'saltimbanque à jeun' whose task is to 'faire épanouir la rate du vulgaire'; in 'La Mort des artistes', where he appears attired with the jingling bells of a jester; while in the much more positive 'Bohémiens en voyage', the emphasis falls upon the freedom, confidence, and strength of the Bohemians and on their communion with the deep forces of nature. The literary representation of the artist has been very finely studied by Enid Welsford, and more recently in a European context by Jean Starobinski in *Portrait de l'artiste en saltimbanque.*[43] The high incidence of the artist as mountebank or clown can be said to correspond to a crisis in nineteenth-century culture where the artist appears as an outcast, out of sympathy with society and the prevailing ideology, and clinging or aspiring to an ideal which is hopelessly unreal and in which he cannot ultimately believe. Consequently, he lives out this impossible and contradictory position as a fool. From the figure of fun that he originally was in the *commedia dell'arte*, the fool has become, like the Don Quixote of Daumier or Unamuno, the representative of the problematical state of European culture. It is, I believe, highly significant that the references to the poet as fool are relatively few and slight in *Les Fleurs du Mal*, and much more developed and thematically important in the prose poems. The shift possibly reflects a feeling of failure after the trial of 1857, and also a feeling of social defeat together with increasing fears about the waning of his creative powers after 1861. Charles Mauron[44] identifies the triumph of the social self over the creative artist, to which one might add doubts about the nature and function of art and an inability to believe in the reality of higher truths or values than those degraded ones which constitute the credo of the majority.

In this respect, the contrast between 'Bohémiens en voyage' and 'Le Vieux Saltimbanque' is significant. The Bohemians are in harmony with nature and other cosmic forces. Just as the mothers give to their young 'le trésor toujours prêt des mamelles pendantes', so also the mother goddess Cybele provides nourishment for the adult Bohemians:

> Cybèle, qui les aime, augmente ses verdures,
> Fait couler le rocher et fleurir le désert
> Devant ces voyageurs, pour lesquels est ouvert
> L'empire familier des ténèbres futures.

The emphasis is upon bountiful provision within a kind of terrestrial paradise or promised land. As in the engraving by Callot which inspired it, there is confidence in the future, in time, and, as it were, in space also, which seems to open up in front of the 'tribu prophétique', whose ardent eyes denote optimism and a belief in life. It is only where their gaze turns heavenwards that their eyes become weighed 'par le morne regret des chimères absentes', indicating that their quest is not for some transcendent ideal situated beyond space and time, but for a paradise of which they seem to retain some vague collective memory, and which seems to be promised by the 'empire familier des ténèbres futures'. The whole poem is suffused with a sense of a paradise which is about to be regained, as if the travellers, surrounded by propitious signs, were at any moment about to find what Rimbaud was later to refer to as 'le lieu et la formule'[45] of their quest.

The forward movement of the poem contrasts very sharply with the stasis of 'Le Vieux Saltimbanque'; we see him 'voûté, caduc, décrépit, une ruine d'homme, adossé contre un des poteaux de sa cahute'. The Bohemians form a group, whereas the mountebank, like the 'étranger', is without friends, family, or children. He has no confidence and no hope. 'Il avait renoncé, il avait abdiqué. Sa destinée était faite.' In the one poem, there is movement, exuberance, youth, health, confidence in the future, mystery: in the other immobility, feebleness, old age, solitude, despair amidst the clamour of vanity fair. The 'saltimbanque' is, we are told, the picture of the 'vieil homme de lettres qui a survécu à la génération dont il fut le brillant amuseur [. . .] dans la baraque de qui le monde oublieux ne veut plus entrer'; so that the emphasis seems to fall principally on the social isolation of the poet who no longer has the power to attract a new generation, and the deep, unforgettable look which he casts on the bright lights and the crowds shows his awareness of the relative and transient nature of success, and the inevitable withering of talent and the ingratitude of the public. But in that case, what are we to make of the implied comparison of the fairground with the literary public? We are told that the baraques 'se faisaient une concurrence formidable'. Are we to understand that the 'saltimbanque' and the poet-observer are casting an envious look at the successful who are unconscious of the fate which awaits them? Or are we not rather to understand that, as in 'La Muse vénale', there is a direct criticism of the essence of art itself—that it is a mere diversion, in which the poet himself no longer believes, and whose sole function is to 'faire épanouir la rate du vulgaire'? The poet-saltimbanque, as his comic rags finally testify, is a mere buffoon whose inglorious task, which he has outlived, is to amuse, so that the poem can be read as showing not just the vanity of success, but of art itself.

'Le Fou et la Vénus' presents a number of similarities with 'Le Vieux Saltimbanque', and it contrasts with 'Bohémiens en voyage'. The Bohemians are in harmony with the external world, whereas the fool is an 'être affligé' in the midst of the exuberance and delight of all things. Like the 'saltimbanque' he, too, finds himself in a kind of festival:

L'extase universelle des choses ne s'exprime par aucun bruit; les eaux elles-mêmes sont comme endormies. Bien différentes des fêtes humaines, c'est ici une orgie silencieuse.
On dirait qu'une lumière toujours croissante fait de plus en plus étinceler les objets.

Not for the fool 'l'amour du repos et le sentiment du bonheur qu'inspire une immense lumière' which Baudelaire celebrates in the *Salon* of 1859.[46] Out of harmony with men and with nature, he appears at his most ridiculous, devoid of dignity and prestige, 'un de ces fous artificiels, un de ces bouffons volontaires chargés de faire rire les rois quand le Remords ou l'Ennui les obsède, affublé d'un costume éclatant et ridicule, coiffé de cornes et de sonnettes'. As in Mallarmé's 'Les Fenêtres', the rift between poet and ideal is total, and the alternative is the degrading task of providing amusement for a bored and tyrannical prince. However, in one sense the poem provides a less disturbing view of the poet-creator who, although a fool, continues to have some belief in a higher form of art than that which he provides for the consumption of the vulgar, and to aspire to an understanding of the nature of beauty. In spite of the indifference of the goddess, whose blank marble eyes look vaguely into the distance,[47] unlike those in the related poem 'La Beauté' in *Les Fleurs du Mal*, which are 'de purs miroirs qui font toutes choses plus belles', and in spite of the sense of a threatened defeat, which is also present in 'La Beauté', one detects a positive value in the aspiration itself, independently of any belief in the possibility of his even creating the kind of art he envisages. In the light of this, it would seem gratuitous and trivializing to see the poem, as some critics have,[48] as representing Baudelaire's relationship with women and to detect in it the veiled presence of sexual inadequacy.

However, the most profound and complex examination of the problematic status of art and the artist is to be found in 'Une mort héroïque', possibly the most successful and fascinating of the prose poems, and one which has been brilliantly explicated by Jean Starobinski, Ch. Mauron, and Ross Chambers.[49] There is uncertainty in this poem about the nature of the buffoon or *histrion* who also feels attracted to the revolutionary ideals of freedom and patriotism. Fancioulle appears immediately as the serious fool, rash enough to enter into a plot against his protector the tyrannical prince whose favourite he is. It has been suggested that he represents an aspect of Baudelaire's own temperament, reflected in the 'Pauvre chantre des *Orfraies*',[50] the Samuel Cramer of *La Fanfarlo* who in his degeneracy founds a socialist newspaper, and in the poet's somewhat farcical involvement on the barricades in the 1848 revolution. This may well be the case, though it is not altogether clear what the relevance of a purely political revolt would be for the buffoon-artist of the poem. The idea would appear to be that his idealism overflows into social action, as if it might be possible to create or restore a better society. Such a belief would of course be very far removed from the mature Baudelaire's views on the reality of original sin and the vanity of the notion of progress, but it would not be incompatible with the proposition that he continued to feel a nostalgia for his youthful political idealism long after the collapse of his dreams at the time of the *coup d'état*. It would, on the other hand, be quite unsatisfactory to interpret the buffoon's revolt and the subsequent death sentence merely as the poet's device to justify the prince's desire to find out how far the intoxication of art can cover up the terrors of death and of the abyss. Another possibility would be to interpret the revolt as representing the serious side of the poet's dual nature, the one which is bent upon action in the real world rather than dream and illusion, and, which he tells us, he was aware of from childhood: 'Étant enfant, je voulais être tantôt pape, mais pape militaire, tantôt comédien.'[51] Also, it is well known that Baudelaire was obsessed from an early age with paradoxes, such as the seriousness of comedy and the comedy of tragedy, which are, of course, manifestations of the many dualities which lie at the centre of his world vision. In the context of the poem itself, the most compelling interpretation would perhaps be to see the revolt, not so much as a political or social phenomenon, but in more general terms as a revolt against the established order of the prince, the idea being that art is by nature subversive, since it presents a world which is fundamentally different from any accepted norm. Fancioulle's mistake is to confuse his metaphysical or artistic revolt with the aims of the conspiring gentlemen he aligns himself with. Furthermore, the paradox concerning seriousness and buffoonery is not presented in political terms in the poem, but within the very art of the *histrion*. We learn that he excelled in those 'drames féeriques dont l'objet est de représenter symboliquement le mystère de la vie', and that he manages to introduce 'le divin et le surnaturel, jusque dans les plus extravagantes bouffonneries'. Accordingly, we have the curious double role of the artist, reduced here to the silent eloquence of the mime, which is at the same time to entertain as fool, and also to represent the mystery of life[52] as do the greatest creators such as Hugo, Delacroix, and indeed Baudelaire himself.

    The buffoon's name, Fancioulle, is also highly significant. It is, of course, the Italian word for child, and Baudelaire must certainly have chosen it 'en connaissance de cause'; for in his poetic universe the artist is related not just to the buffoon, but even more importantly to the child. In *Le Peintre de la vie moderne* he defined genius as 'l'*enfance retrouvée* à volonté'.[53] The child is always drunk and, consequently, will not feel 'l'horrible fardeau du temps'. Indeed, in the 'vert paradis des amours enfantines' of *Les Fleurs du Mal*,[54] the implication is that the poet-child has escaped, at least subjectively, from time and that he sees the world not through the disenchanted eyes of the adult, but as fascinating and bathed in glory. He sees 'la vie en beau', and these various elements associated with childhood—timelessness, fascination, glory, the reintegration of paradise—are all present in 'Une mort héroïque':

l'ivresse de l'Art est plus apte que toute autre à voiler les terreurs du gouffre;
[. . .] le génie peut jouer la comédie au bord de la tombe avec une joie qui

l'empêche de voir la tombe, perdu, comme il est, dans un paradis excluant toute idée de tombe et de destruction.

We are told that on the fateful evening Fancioulle excelled as never before in his art, and that he was a perfect idealization which had somehow come to life: 'Ce bouffon allait, venait, riait, pleurait, se convulsait' with the result that the normally frivolous and blasé prince and audience burst out in explosions of laughter and thunderous applause. What is extraordinary in the poem, as well as typical of the whole aesthetic of dissonance which presides over the prose poems, is the way in which the effects of this more or less dumb pantomime, which causes so much violent laughter, are equated to those of high culture and the most serious art. The grotesque of a pantomime is equated to the sublime of such pieces from *Les Fleurs du Mal* as 'La Chevelure' or 'Le Balcon'. Fancioulle's performance has quite rightly been compared to a passage in *De l'essence du rire*, where Baudelaire describes the English pantomime which he had seen in Paris, and which he gives as an example of the grotesque and of the 'comique absolu'.

Aussitôt le vertige est entré, le vertige circule dans l'air; on respire le vertige; c'est le vertige qui remplit les poumons et renouvelle le sang dans le ventricule. Qu'est-ce que le vertige? C'est le comique absolu; il s'est emparé de chaque être. Léandre, Pierrot, Cassandre, font des gestes extraordinaires, qui démontrent clairement qu'ils se sentent introduits de force dans une existence nouvelle [. . .] Et ils s'élancent à travers l'œuvre fantastique, qui, à proprement parler, ne commence que là, c'est-à-dire sur la frontière du merveilleux.[55]

Given Fancioulle's attainment of the 'comique absolu', which Baudelaire sees as having 'quelque chose de profond, d'axiomatique et de primitif qui se rapproche beaucoup plus de la vie innocente et de la joie absolue que le rire causé par le comique des mœurs',[56] it might seem at first sight that the contention about the problematic nature of the artist and more particularly of his art in this poem must be unsound; for, until he is interrupted, Fancioulle, unlike the fool in 'Le Fou et la Vénus' and 'Le Vieux Saltimbanque', is successful, and the 'coup de sifflet'[57] which is ordered by the prince, killing him in the middle of his act, is merely the foolish and gratuitous experiment of an unthinking and philistine witness. Whereas the poet's halo[58] had simply fallen off as he crossed the street, the fool's invisible and indestructible one stays with him even in death; and this is, no doubt, because his art, like great poetry, is 'essentiellement *bête*'; it has the faith and belief which are its splendour and strength;[59] or, as Baudelaire has it in the *Salon* of 1859, 'le poète, le comédien et l'artiste, au moment où ils exécutent l'ouvrage en question, croient à la réalité de ce qu'ils représentent, échauffés qu'ils sont par la nécessité'.[60] In the paradise of his art, excluding any idea of death or destruction, the buffoon is at one with his role and accedes momentarily to a fullness of being which seems to deny the divisions of everyday experience which cause men to be spectators of themselves.[61] But the objection is soon set aside, since in 'Une mort héroïque', with its gratingly ironic title, the artist is still only a fool, his art a mere 'drame féerique', and the veiling of the abyss is illusory. Art is indeed fundamentally lacking in seriousness, even when it claims, or is thought to represent, the mystery of life; it is a lie, a Pascalian 'divertissement' concealing from men the realities of their condition. Since, as La Rochefoucauld has it, 'le soleil ni la mort ne se peuvent regarder fixement',[62] the discourse of art, far from bearing witness to the power and grandeur of the human mind, resembles nothing as much as the vain prattle of those empty spirits Baudelaire mentions in 'La Solitude':

> Il y a dans nos races jacassières des individus qui accepteraient avec moins de répugnance le supplice suprême, s'il leur était permis de faire du haut de l'échafaud une copieuse harangue, sans craindre que les tambours de Santerre ne leur coupassent intempestivement la parole.

Worse than the 'histrion en vacances' of 'La Béatrice', and for all his power to express the mystery of life, Fancioulle appears as a charlatan, unable, as Ross Chambers[63] puts it, to bring about the synthesis of art and real experience.

The objection must fall also because of the identity of the tyrannical prince. One recognizes in him certain Baudelairean features; he is a fuller version of the king in 'Le Fou et la Vénus' and of the third 'Spleen' poem of *Les Fleurs du Mal*:

> Je suis comme le roi d'un pays pluvieux, [. . .].
> Rien ne peut l'égayer, ni gibier, ni faucon,
> Ni son peuple mourant en face du balcon.
> Du bouffon favori la grotesque ballade
> Ne distrait plus le front de ce cruel malade.

The prince of 'Une mort héroïque' is like Baudelaire himself, a passionate lover of the arts and 'insatiable de voluptés', indifferent to morality, almost an artist himself, whose worst enemy is ennui; he is a minor Nero, intent upon strong emotions coupled with a certain sadism, in order, like Fancioulle, to escape from the rigours of time and of spleen. Like the narrator of 'Le Mauvais Vitrier', he is representative of the exasperated artist and the frustrated idealist who seeks an illusion of transcendence in the cruel cult of strong emotions. *His* revolt is against the naïvety and innocence of the childlike buffoon and against the ultimate insubstantiality of his art, the only alternatives to which are mediocre eclecticism,[64] silence, or violence. He chooses the latter. Totally different from the philistine public Baudelaire castigates elsewhere, he is, in fact, the negative side of the poet himself, the cynic, the realist, the disbeliever. So that the lesson of the poem is that lucidity kills the artist, cynicism kills inspiration, realism kills 'ivresse', or, in the words of Charles Mauron,[65] the super-ego and the social self kill the deep self and the poet.

The split in the poetic persona is further aggravated by the presence of the narrator, who is not just a detached observer as in some of the other pieces, but is emotionally involved in the spectacle and the outcome of the action. His pen trembles and hysterical tears come to his eyes as he tries to describe that unforgettable evening, with the result that the poem exemplifies most convincingly on the level of personality that thematic fragmentation which has already been noted in connection with the collection as a whole; for Baudelaire is Fancioulle, the prince, and the narrator at the same time.

This split in the poetic persona, or, rather, this fragmentation of personality, is a powerful characteristic of the prose poems, distinguishing them once again from *Les Fleurs du Mal*, where it is less developed, and where almost all of the poems are presented with the voice of the poet or artist. This is not to suggest that Baudelaire did not find various figures in *Les Fleurs du Mal* to represent his many moods and convictions. 'Don Juan aux enfers', 'Bohémiens en voyage', possibly even the 'Femmes damnées' can all be seen as proof of the contrary, and, indeed, it would be surprising not to find such personae in a collection in which he sought to discover objective correlatives, as T. S. Eliot called them,[66] of his states of soul, and to make of such mundane objects as scent bottles, cemeteries, and cracked church bells, the vehicles of the emotion in his poems. The incidence of such figures is particularly marked in 'Tableaux parisiens', only eight of which existed in the first edition, where they were grouped with the poems of 'Spleen et Idéal', there being no separate section in the 1857 edition. The human ruins which he calls his family in 'Les Petites Vieilles', and which are clearly extensions of himself,[67] are much more numerous in 'Tableaux parisiens' and the prose poems. Baudelaire's identification with, for example, widows, the poor, 'les monstres innocents', in short, with all the solitary, rejected, and misunderstood, with the 'éclopés de la vie',[68] would appear to be a developing feature of his art. The split in personality reveals itself in *Les Fleurs du Mal* as a kind of empathy with the unfortunate (there is no identification with the rich, overfed, and successful), as a nightmarish vision in which he sees himself in some low gambling den 'accoudé, froid, muet, enviant,/Enviant de ces gens la passion tenace',[69] or as a statement in 'L'Héautontimorouménos', rather than a demonstration, that he is both victim and torturer:

> Je suis la plaie et le couteau!
> Je suis le soufflet et la joue!
> Je suis les membres et la roue,
> Et la victime et le bourreau!

But in the prose poems the poet does not only seek out those whose solitude and misfortune resemble his in a general way; rather he gives life to personae who represent whole aspects of his artistic personality and who often are incompatible with one another, so that he is the old mountebank, each one of the dandies in 'Portraits de maîtresses', the observer and the observed, the detached and the involved commentator, the prince and the buffoon, the 'mauvais vitrier' and the exasperated aesthete who assaults him, the victim and the torturer.

'Les Vocations' is an excellent example of the fragmentation of the poetic personality within one poem. It relates the conversation of four little boys in a fine garden on an autumn evening at sunset; each one talks in turn about an experience which has obsessed him to such an extent that it will act in his life as a vocation, leading him ultimately towards renown or dishonour. The first boy tells of his visit to the theatre, the second, whom we have already met in the discussion of 'L'Étranger', sees God on a cloud, the third describes how once on holiday, there being no room at the inn, he spent the night in the family maid's bed, and the fourth how he overhears the conversation of some Bohemians and doesn't have the courage to ask to go with them. Although it is significant that at the end of the poem, Baudelaire, the observer, should identify himself most closely with the boy who wants to be a Bohemian, entertaining the bizarre idea 'que je pouvais avoir un frère à moi-même inconnu', it is clear that he is all the children of the piece, experiencing equally and simultaneously the theatrical, mystical, erotic, and Bohemian vocations, each one of which is a powerful theme in both the verse and the prose poems.[70]

Now at the beginning of 'Les Foules' Baudelaire explains that two qualities are necessary to enable him to identify himself with others and to take the famous 'bain de multitude', and these are firstly, 'le goût du travestissement et du masque', and secondly, 'la haine du domicile et la passion du voyage'. That is, in order to make that 'sainte prostitution de l'âme qui se donne tout entière, poésie et charité, à l'imprévu qui se montre, à l'inconnu qui passe', the poet needs to fulfil two of the vocations of the piece of that name; he has to have the vocation of the comedian-actor and of the Bohemian. The actor's vocation will provide him with the mask which will enable him to pass incognito in the midst of the crowd, since the poet-'flâneur' is a *prince* qui jouit partout de son incognito'; but, more than that, it will allow him to épouser la foule' in much the same way as the actor can enter into the mind, body, and character of the role he is playing. It will give him that kind of artistic 'disponibilité', to use Gide's terminology, which is the property of great actors, and which Baudelaire was able to admire in Philibert Rouvière.[71] Similarly, the Bohemian vocation with its rejection of fixed patterns, stultifying convention, and introspection, opens the poetic mind to the solicitations of the outside world within the bustle and commotion of the big city in much the same way as the Bohemians in the prose poem and in 'Bohémiens en voyage' are open to the grandeur of the natural world; so that the poet's voyeurism is linked to his need to travel and to the theme of 'le voyage'. It is as if the poet were experiencing in the crowds of the city an emotion analogous to pantheism: 'Le vertige senti dans les grandes villes est analogue au vertige éprouvé au sein de la nature. — Délices du chaos et de l'immensité.'[72] The link between 'Les Vocations' and 'Les Foules' is clear and inescapable; they are linked by the themes of the theatre and escape from the restrictions of habit. The following

crucial passage from *Le Peintre de la vie moderne* casts further light
on this mental attitude:

> La foule est son domaine, comme l'air est celui de l'oiseau, comme l'eau
> celui du poisson. Sa passion et sa profession, c'est d'*épouser la foule*. Pour
> le parfait flâneur, pour l'observateur passionné, c'est une immense jouissance
> que d'élire domicile dans le nombre, dans l'ondoyant, dans le mouvement,
> dans le fugitif et l'infini. Être hors de chez soi, et pourtant se sentir partout
> chez soi; voir le monde, être au centre du monde et rester caché au monde,
> tels sont quelques-uns des moindres plaisirs de ces esprits indépendants,
> passionnés, impartiaux, que la langue ne peut que maladroitement définir.
> L'observateur est un *prince* qui jouit partout de son incognito. L'amateur
> de la vie fait du monde sa famille, comme l'amateur du beau sexe compose
> sa famille de toutes les beautés trouvées, trouvables et introuvables; comme
> l'amateur de tableaux vit dans une société enchantée de rêves peints sur la
> toile. Ainsi l'amoureux de la vie universelle entre dans la foule comme dans
> un immense réservoir d'électricité.[73]

But what of the other two vocations, the sexual and the religious?
Are they also essential for the successful 'bain de multitude', the
ability to lose oneself in others; and can the links between the two
prose poems be broadened and strengthened, so that they can be
thought of as complementary? This would indeed appear to be
the case; for the passage from the self to the other, as the above
quotation from the study on Constantin Guys has hinted, with its
reference to the lover of women and the lover of life, is described
in 'Les Foules' in overtly sexual terms, as a prostitution, a 'ribote
de vitalité', as an 'ineffable orgie'. And if one turns to the passage
in 'Les Tentations' where Baudelaire describes the temptation of Eros,
one might be forgiven for thinking he is talking about crowds,
because Satan promises that the poet will find, in succumbing to
Eros, 'le plaisir, sans cesse renaissant, de sortir de toi-même pour
t'oublier dans autrui, et d'attirer les autres âmes jusqu'à les confondre
avec la tienne'. The expression 'épouser la foule' is no dead metaphor,
since the link the poet establishes with the crowd is a quasi-sexual
one, and he will know, the poet tells us with a gentle touch of
irony, the same compensations as missionary priests and founders
of colonies, who experience similar exaltations and who must laugh
at those who pity them on account of their 'fortune si agitée et
[. . .] leur vie si chaste'. The disproportion in such a comparison
is sufficient to provoke a wry smile, but not to undermine the moral
message of the poem.

It is interesting and typical that in *Le Spleen de Paris* real relationships with wife or mistress are intolerable, as, for example, in 'La Soupe et les nuages', 'La Femme sauvage et la petite-maîtresse', 'Le Galant Tireur', and 'Les Yeux des pauvres', while the quasi-sexual link with the crowd is fulfilling. The most moving and the most successful of the relationships the poet establishes with other people is to be found in 'Les Veuves', which adds a real sexual element to the quasi-sexual, since the young widow, this 'Singulière vision' who becomes an allegorical figure of loneliness and disproportion, is clearly morally and physically attractive. She is the saddest kind of widow, since she is forced to trail with her 'un bambin avec qui elle ne peut pas partager sa rêverie':

C'était une femme grande, majestueuse, et si noble dans tout son air, que je n'ai pas souvenir d'avoir vu sa pareille dans les collections des aristocratiques beautés du passé. Un parfum de hautaine vertu émanait de toute sa personne.

Like the widow of 'A une passante' in *Les Fleurs du Mal*, 'Longue, mince, en grand deuil, douleur majestueuse', she is a solitary, aristocratic, and intense figure. Whatever the origins of Baudelaire's preoccupation with widows, which critics have not failed to link with his own ambivalent attitudes towards his own mother, it seems clear that his fascination for them can be explained because, like all the unfortunate and bereaved, they appear to him as representations of his 'irrémédiable existence'.[74] There is also in this prose poem, as in 'A une passante' an element, I'd suggest, of what Walter Benjamin has very aptly called 'love at last sight'.[75] The love affair which is suggested gains its prestige from its virtuality; the ennobling outward signs of beauty and virtue are imperishable, since they will never be put to the test of real experience and will remain limited to an instant, which is poised for ever between a past in whose depths happiness has been lost and a future which can never be realized.

For the links between 'Les Foules' and 'Les Vocations' to be complete, it remains to discuss the vocation of the second little boy, who sees God on a cloud. What can the religious vocation and the identification of the poet with other people have in common? It is immediately apparent that Baudelaire talks of the poet's prostitution in religious terms; it is a 'sainte prostitution' which gives itself 'poésie et charité, à l'imprévu qui se montre, à l'inconnu qui passe'; and in his *Journaux intimes* he writes that God is 'l'être le plus prostitué',

since he is 'l'ami suprême pour chaque individu, puisqu'il est le
réservoir commun, inépuisable de l'amour',[76] and since love, being
made of the desire to get out of oneself and sacrifice oneself for
others, is also a form of prostitution: 'L'amour, c'est le goût de la
prostitution. Il n'est même pas de plaisir noble qui ne puisse être
ramené à la Prostitution.'[77] But he also declares that *art is
prostitution*,[78] so that what we are witnessing in the 'Tableaux
parisiens' and *Le Spleen de Paris* is a kind of artistic selflessness or
prostitution which, taking the poet out of the closed self-sufficiency
of the dandy, enables him, it would appear, to respond charitably
to the appeal of the outside world and to enter the minds and feelings
of those whom he encounters in the course of his 'flânerie'. It is as
if the poet were responding aesthetically (and morally) to Flaubert's
injunction to 'se transporter dans les personnages, et non les attirer
à soi',[79] in order to create an impersonal art in place of the personal
effusions of the Romantics. It emerges that 'Les Vocations' is not
merely a random grouping of four sensitive little boys, but is a
profound meditation on the nature of art and the temperament of
the artist.

   However, this outward movement which is celebrated in 'Les
Foules' and 'Les Vocations' is counterbalanced by an opposite
movement inwards, of concentration upon the self in a solitude
which, at least in some poems, appears satisfying; so that 'Les Foules'
is balanced by 'La Solitude' where Baudelaire pours scorn upon all
those who affirm in humanitarian clichés that solitude is bad for men,
showing thereby their superficiality, idle curiosity, and spiritual
nullity. In favour of solitude he quotes, not without a suspicion of
irony to which we shall return, the great moralists of the classical
period, La Bruyère and, in particular, Pascal:

'Presque tous nos malheurs nous viennent de n'avoir pas su rester dans
notre chambre', dit un autre sage, Pascal, je crois, rappelant ainsi dans la
cellule du recueillement tous ces affolés qui cherchent le bonheur dans le
mouvement et dans une prostitution que je pourrais appeler *fraternitaire*,
si je voulais parler la belle langue de mon siècle.

Here we have an immediate contrast with the 'sainte prostitution'
of 'Les Foules', with Baudelaire's irony falling once more on the
Utopian humanists of his time and their belief in progress, liberty,
equality, fraternity, and the creation of perfect societies. Like Balzac,
for whom established religion had as its principal function the

repression of the depraved instincts of men, like Flaubert, obsessed with human stupidity and folly, Baudelaire, under the influence of Joseph de Maistre, subscribes to a pessimistic view of mankind, believing that the only progress can lie in the diminution of original sin. There is much of Pascal's Jansenism in Baudelaire, who shares the view that men are unable to remain in their room for fear of being confronted with the realities of their condition and with their own nullity. Consequently, they seek distraction in the frivolities of court life or in hunting, whereas only religion and the redemption of Christ will enable us to look upon the human condition with any kind of equanimity.

However, in 'La Solitude' Baudelaire gives no indication of the nature and substance of his meditation. He suggests that solitude would be dangerous to the 'âme oisive et divagante qui la peuple de ses passions et de ses chimères', and the implication is clearly that he is not such a man; but in other prose poems he does indulge in such day-dreams and empty fantasies, and there is little evidence anywhere in his work of the Christian notion of salvation or grace. The result is that 'La Solitude' would appear to correspond to an undefined or unattainable ideal of 'recueillement' rather than to the reality, or it is perhaps intended to lead to one of the poet's habitual 'examens de conscience'. Its function may be to form a contrast with that degraded prostitution which is made only of a desire for movement and change, and which tries to dignify itself by the spurious notion of fraternity with other people. In that case, its function would appear to be negative, rather than positive, to provide a haven from the stridency and vulgarity of the outside world. 'La Solitude' would then have much in common with 'A une heure du matin', where the poet seeks refuge from the tyranny of the human face, from the abrasive contact with the stupidity, ignorance, arrogance, and hypocrisy of his 'bêtes noires', such as directors of theatres and reviews, and 'sauteuses' wishing him to draw a costume of 'Vénustre'. He laments that he has distributed handshakes indiscriminately without taking the precaution of buying gloves. Contact with such a base reality has not just rubbed his sensibility the wrong way, but it has alienated him from his true self, with the result that he adopts a mask of cynicism, indifference, and immorality. Solitude is, therefore, necessary for him to reintegrate the self which has not been deformed or corrupted by the vulgar world.

There is, then, in the prose poems a typical thematic oscillation between solitude and 'sainte prostitution', between concentration upon self and dispersion into the outside world of objects or people. It is possibly this movement that Baudelaire is referring to somewhat enigmatically in 'Mon cœur mis à nu', when he states: 'De la vaporisation et de la centralisation du *Moi*. Tout est là.'[80] The vaporization takes place in the poems where he transports himself into the outside world or into other personae; the centralization is evident in the moments of introspection or of an 'examen de conscience', such as 'La Solitude' or 'A une heure du matin'. But the two movements need not necessarily be incompatible or confined to separate poems. In 'Le *Confiteor* de l'artiste', for example, there is a coming and going between the inside world of the poet and the outside world of sea, sky, and autumn sunset:

> Grand délice que celui de noyer son regard dans l'immensité du ciel et de la mer! Solitude, silence, incomparable chasteté de l'azur! une petite voile frissonnante à l'horizon, et qui par sa petitesse et son isolement imite mon irrémédiable existence, mélodie monotone de la houle, toutes ces choses pensent par moi, ou je pense par elles (car dans la grandeur de la rêverie, le *moi* se perd vite!); elles pensent, dis-je, mais musicalement et pittoresquement, sans arguties, sans syllogismes, sans déductions.
> Toutefois, ces pensées, qu'elles sortent de moi ou s'élancent des choses, deviennent bientôt trop intenses.

In the prose poems the feeling that the separate existence of the self is lost is often indicated by such expressions as 'noyer son regard', 'bain de ténèbres', or 'bain de multitude'. Here, typically, the barrier between subject and object has disappeared, the self is at once vaporized into the outside world and at the same time, having internalized the outside world, is totally concentrated upon itself. The two states of mind are in fact fused and simultaneous, and should not be seen as contradictory, but as complementary.

A similar phenomenon can be seen in 'Déjà!'. While the other passengers show their impatience with the long sea journey and their delight when land is sighted, the poet sighs 'déjà' and is unable to detach himself from his solitary contemplation of the sea:

> de cette mer si infiniment variée dans son effrayante simplicité, et qui semble contenir en elle et représenter par ses jeux, ses allures, ses colères et ses sourires, les humeurs, les agonies et les extases de toutes les âmes qui ont vécu, qui vivent et qui vivront!

The sea appears here as a vast, multiple, and variable metaphor for the many faces of the human soul.[81] As in 'Le *Confiteor* de l'artiste', the thoughts seem to come both from the poet and from the sea itself, and there is the same sense of the poet being lost in his contemplation. One might be tempted to think that solitude is being presented here in entirely positive terms, were it not for the sense of a withdrawal from the real world, which is described in the most prestigious terms as a 'terre riche et magnifique, pleine de promesses', in favour of the kind of vain and insubstantial musings we found in 'L'Étranger'.

In order fully to understand the complementarity of vaporization and centralization, between prostitution and solitude, it is necessary to be aware of the difference between 'prostitution fraternitaire', which is a lax and superficial comradeship based upon curiosity and the inability to be alone, and 'sainte prostitution', which avoids direct involvement, but cultivates contact through empathy and reverie, leading ultimately to a deepening of the poet's experience. The poet is immersed in the crowd as 'flâneur' or 'rôdeur', as the observer who does not participate. His contact with others is visual, not tactile, and he has no need to wear protective gloves. It is essential also that the object of his pity should be anonymous, and unaware that he or she has been singled out by the poet. Once again in this connection, the *Journaux intimes* provide enlightenment. Baudelaire talks of the 'goût invincible de la prostitution' in the heart of man 'd'où naît son horreur de la solitude. — Il veut être *deux*. L'homme de génie veut être *un*, donc solitaire. La gloire, c'est rester *un*, et se prostituer d'une manière particulière.'[82] Though Baudelaire does not explain what that particular manner is, we can surely conclude that it is through his art, not just through its publication (that quasi-prostitution of the self to a philistine and unworthy public),[83] but rather through the ineffable orgy which gives itself to the chance encounters of its urban wanderings. In this way, the poet remains one, while at the same time surrendering to the outside world, but avoiding the fraternal and superficial dilution of the self, so that his experience is ultimately one of an intense self-discovery. The most explicit account of this process is beyond doubt 'Les Fenêtres' where, although there is no crowd, we find the familiar movement from the self to the other and then back to self. It would be helpful to quote the poem in its entirety:

Celui qui regarde du dehors à travers une fenêtre ouverte, ne voit jamais autant de choses que celui qui regarde une fenêtre fermée. Il n'est pas d'objet plus profond, plus mystérieux, plus fécond, plus ténébreux, plus éblouissant qu'une fenêtre éclairée d'une chandelle. Ce qu'on peut voir au soleil est toujours moins intéressant que ce qui se passe derrière une vitre. Dans ce trou noir ou lumineux vit la vie, rêve la vie, souffre la vie.

Par-delà des vagues de toits, j'aperçois une femme mûre, ridée déjà, pauvre, toujours penchée sur quelque chose, et qui ne sort jamais. Avec son visage, avec son vêtement, avec son geste, avec presque rien, j'ai refait l'histoire de cette femme, ou plutôt sa légende, et quelquefois je me la raconte à moi-même en pleurant.

Si c'eût été un pauvre vieux homme, j'aurais refait la sienne tout aussi aisément.

Et je me couche, fier d'avoir vécu et souffert dans d'autres que moi-même.

Peut-être me direz-vous: 'Es-tu sûr que cette légende soit la vraie?' Qu'importe ce que peut être la réalité placée hors de moi, si elle m'a aidé à vivre, à sentir que je suis et ce que je suis?

The poem opens with a paradox: 'Celui qui regarde du dehors à travers une fenêtre ouverte, ne voit jamais autant de choses que celui qui regarde une fenêtre fermée'—which blatantly goes counter to common sense and experience. The poet describes a window with a candle and states that 'Dans ce trou noir ou lumineux vit la vie, rêve la vie, souffre la vie.' It is important to notice that the qualities which bring him close to the unfortunate are, as is implied in other prose poems, intensity, reverie, and suffering. After a splendid image, 'Par-delà des vagues de toits', which not only gives the impression of a turbulent movement in the roof-tops at different levels, but also the impression of the opening up of a distance whereby the real space becomes the subjective space of the mind, the poet claims to have caught sight of a little old woman, reminiscent of the widows and the 'petites vieilles' we have met elsewhere, 'mûre, ridée déjà, pauvre, toujours penchée sur quelque chose et qui ne sort jamais'. With a very few observable traits, some of which are incompatible with the distance between him and the woman's window, the poet is able to reconstruct the history of the woman, or rather her legend, and goes to bed proud that he has lived and suffered in others than himself. The irony is patent, and immediately calls from the possible reader the objection that he cannot be sure the legend corresponds to reality, which draws the characteristically prompt and cavalier riposte from the poet: 'Qu'importe ce que peut être la réalité placée hors de moi, si elle m'a aidé à vivre, à sentir que je suis et ce que je suis?'[84]

The key to the piece is, as the title indicates, the symbol of the window and the distance between the poet and the object he is contemplating. The window functions, after all, as a kind of mirror in which there is some reflection of the poet himself. He is, then, at once looking from outside into the room and into himself. The candle in the room increases the impression of spacial depth and provides contrasts between areas of light and dark, so that what he is looking at stands out, as in a dream or a painting, against a background of darkness. The scene is both 'ténébreux' and 'éblouissant', 'fécond' and 'mystérieux', poor in real detail and rich in detail suggested to the imagination. The surrounding darkness, the paucity of detail, and the blurring of outline transform the real woman into an object rich in suggestion and which, like the paintings of Delacroix or the sketches of Guys, is able to speak to the imagination and, above all, the memory of the poet. The window is, accordingly, the perfect symbol, bringing together inside and outside, dream and reality, self and non-self, and the spectacle, thus perceived, becomes for the poet a means of self-exploration. Through such a prostitution, the poet remains one; vaporization is also at the same time centralization, and the other person is an intense experience and expression of the individual.[85] It seems as though in many of the prose poems Baudelaire is viewing the scenes of Paris life through such a transforming window. Much has been made by some critics of the realism of these poems and by would-be imitators who have produced turgid 'choses vues' of Paris life; but what is most striking is the surreal quality of the poems, and the extent to which they bring about a fusion of poetry and life.

It should, however, be stressed that 'Les Fenêtres' is the only one of the prostitution pieces to sound an ironical note which is so strong as to undermine the exercise in empathy which the poem is supposed to be celebrating: 'Et je me couche, fier d'avoir vécu et souffert dans d'autres que moi-même.' Such irony, which casts doubt on the whole notion of 'sainte prostitution', is totally absent from 'Les Petites Vieilles' with which it provides an enlightening contrast:

> Sombres ou lumineux, je vis vos jours perdus;
> Mon cœur multiplié jouit de tous vos vices!
> Mon âme resplendit de toutes vos vertus!

'Les Foules', 'Les Veuves', 'Le Vieux Saltimbanque', and even 'Les Yeux des pauvres' have, in spite of their melancholy subject-matter, a vitality, an intensity, and, above all, a genuine and unquestioned pity which is maintained to the end, whereas the 'solitude' pieces, such as 'Le Confiteor de l'artiste' and 'La Chambre double', start with a spiritual intensity and vitality, the élan of which cannot be maintained: the inspiration fails, the dream dissolves, the dreaded reality returns, and once again, as in 'Une mort héroïque', we witness the sad experience of the disappointing nature of art which is able only momentarily to conceal the terrors of the abyss. In 'Le Confiteor' the very intensity of the dream is the cause of its evanescence as the poet's nerves are not strong enough to maintain the vision:

L'énergie dans la volupté crée un malaise et une souffrance positive. Mes nerfs trop tendus ne donnent plus que des vibrations criardes et douloureuses. Et maintenant la profondeur du ciel me consterne; sa limpidité m'exaspère.

The nerves cannot maintain the tension. Nature, the rival of art and its temptress, is victorious. 'L'étude du beau est un duel où l'artiste crie de frayeur avant d'être vaincu.' Defeat is once more the lot of the artist, as in 'Le Fou et la Vénus' and 'Une mort héroïque', because of the insufficiencies within the artist and because of the problematical nature of art itself. 'Le Confiteor' is, consequently, more pessimistic than 'La Chambre double' which has many parallels with 'Une mort héroïque', such as the emphasis on timelessness, 'ivresse', a beatific vision, and the veiling of the terrors of the abyss. But in 'La Chambre double' the dream fails only because of the intrusion of the outside world, the knock on the door bringing the demands of the real world and society. The knock, bringing bailiff or demanding concubine, is, in a sense, similar to the whistle in 'Une mort héroïque' which came, of course, from the cruel prince, alter ego of the poet bent on an interesting experiment with life, death, and art. In 'Le Confiteor' the defeat is all the greater for the initial success, and since it stems from an inadequacy within the poet, and not from any intrusion of the outside world.

The predominantly gloomy view of art and of the artist which has emerged in this chapter is open to one very telling and fundamental objection: how can it be reconciled with the positive function of art which is the theme of 'Le Thyrse', probably the best known and most quoted of the prose poems and, what is more important, the one which, in the opinion of many critics such as Lemaître, is thought to be symbolic of the relationship of prose and poetry and to constitute 'l'image mythologique qui figure exactement son art'?[86] Barbara Johnson has expressed considerable disquiet at such an interpretation, and her 'deconstructive' reading completely upsets Lemaître's, so that 'Le Thyrse' appears not so much as a model of Baudelaire's prose poetry, but rather as 'une mise en abyme infinie de sa propre incapacité à servir de modèle'.[87] Whatever reservations[88] one may have about such a reading, this reconsideration of what is largely an unargued critical commonplace which has been taken for granted, is welcome and refreshing. Lemaître's view does not take sufficiently into account that the poem is first and foremost a homage to the musical talent of Liszt, to whom it is dedicated and who is addressed throughout the poem. That Baudelaire had for many years been fascinated by the figure of the thyrsus, and had exploited it to admirable effect in 'Le Serpent qui danse',[89] should not lead us to the hasty conclusion that it is relevant to all his literary production. The union of opposites which the poem celebrates may well be applicable to many of the *Fleurs du Mal*, and it is certainly relevant to the romantic and undulating harmonies of Liszt's musical outpourings, which seem to find an echo in the final apostrophe of the piece:

Cher Liszt, à travers les brumes, par-delà les fleuves, par-dessus les villes où les pianos chantent votre gloire, où l'imprimerie traduit votre sagesse, en quelque lieu que vous soyez, dans les splendeurs de la ville éternelle ou dans les brumes des pays rêveurs que console Cambrinus, improvisant des chants de délectation ou d'ineffable douleur, ou confiant au papier vos méditations abstruses, chantre de la Volupté et de l'Angoisse éternelles, philosophe, poète et artiste, je vous salue en l'immortalité!

However, in 'Le Thyrse' there is no hint of the disagreeable moral message[90] which Baudelaire saw as one of the fundamental aims of his prose poetry, no trace of the aesthetic of dissonance or of the disturbing 'soubresaut de la conscience', or of the irony which bends back upon the piece to undermine its harmony of thought or expression. It celebrates an aesthetic which fuses the opposites of male and female, intention and expression, and, above all, fantasy and the controlling power of the intellect. Fantasy, which is dangerous like any other total freedom,[91] is domesticated and given direction by the poet's will and intellect, which, without fantasy and its explosive creativity, would be disappointingly austere and lacking in suggestive power. One is thus led to conclude that the style and verbal texture of the piece together with its optimistic view of art as the harmonious union of opposites, make it, like the 'bagatelle'[92] 'Les Bons Chiens' which Baudelaire wrote for the painter Joseph Stevens in return for the gift of his coveted waistcoat, an exception amid the strident ambiguities of *Le Spleen de Paris*.

II

'Une morale désagréable'

It was Baudelaire's stated intention in *Le Spleen de Paris* to emphasize
the random and accidental aspects of his thought and inspiration and
to draw, or to give the impression of drawing, from his observation
of Paris street scenes through the disillusioned eyes of a man afflicted
by the ennui of a vast modern capital, an unpleasant moral lesson.
His intention, as we have seen, was to show another Joseph Delorme,
without the languor and the elegant melancholy, but with the added
qualities of irony, bitterness, and modernity, 'accrochant sa pensée
rapsodique à chaque accident de sa flânerie et tirant de chaque objet
une morale désagréable',[1] an intention which, though enunciated as
late as 1866, becomes increasingly obvious in the various alternative
titles he envisaged for the collection: *Poèmes nocturnes*, *La Lueur
et la fumée*, *Le Promeneur solitaire*, *Le Rôdeur parisien*, *Le Flâneur
des deux rives*. There is, consequently, in many of the prose poems,
which bear witness to that fascination with crowds and urban
life which Baudelaire admired in Hugo, Poe, and Constantin Guys,
a strong sense of the fortuitous or accidental, the feeling that the
poet just happens to be there and, by a chance turn of his random
wandering through the capital, is vouchsafed, in the observation of
an apparently trivial occurrence, a glimpse into a more significant
and deeper reality. It is as if, through the encounter with the trivial,
some secret truth is revealed, so that if the poet often appears
in the role of a voyeur, his voyeurism is not limited to the petty
trivialities which normally remain unnoticed, but gives on to a
deeper understanding of things. It is a voyeurism which might
be thought of as the moral equivalent of that most poetic of all
faculties, 'voyance'. Since 'la vie parisienne est féconde en sujets
poétiques et merveilleux', and since 'le merveilleux nous enveloppe
et nous abreuve comme l'atmosphère',[2] the result is that the 'choses
vues' tend to take on the power and significance of symbolic or
allegorical figures. One of the finest examples is 'Les Veuves' which,

on the very simplest level, appears little more than a list of the various types of widow that can be seen in the streets or gardens of Paris, until the evocation of the central figure, 'un être dont la noblesse faisait un éclatant contraste avec toute la trivialité environnante'. He describes the 'parfum de hautaine vertu' and the sad, gaunt face of this 'femme grande, majestueuse, et si noble dans tout son air, que je n'ai pas souvenir d'avoir vu sa pareille . . .' until the figure becomes so detached from the base and ignoble surroundings that it becomes a 'Singulière vision' standing above the rest of humanity and endowed with a heightened significance. The moment in which the poet catches sight of her seems, as in 'A une passante', to stand outside time, and this heightening of reality transforms the widow from a 'chose vue' into an allegorical figure of loneliness and disproportion. Or take the mountebank in 'Le Vieux Saltimbanque' who is not just a sad old man whose act has ceased to draw the public; he has become the incarnation of the once successful writer whose message is no longer acceptable or of interest to a public bent on the most strident and mindless 'divertissements'.

But not all such 'choses vues' are as successful. There can, as in 'Un plaisant', be a gap which is difficult to overcome between the description, in this case the splendidly vigorous and chaotic 'explosion' of the New Year, and the moral significance which the poet wishes to attach to it. The 'beau monsieur' who wishes the donkey a happy new year in the middle of the street somehow fails to be elevated to a representative figure of the spirit of France. Whereas the correlation between the mountebank and the poet was immediately perceptible and rich in possible associations and resonances, that between the 'magnifique imbécile' and 'tout l'esprit de la France' seems poor, and indeed seems to detract from the vivid street scene, a veritable 'croquis parisien' worthy of Constantin Guys, having such an immediate appeal to the reader's imagination and memory as to be able to stand on its own without its spurious and. redundant crutches.[3] The moral lesson—that France is composed of vain and useless imbeciles who scoff at the humble and useful who are themselves driven by gross, barbarous, and cruel taskmasters—is unlikely to impress itself on the mind as a great and profound truth. Perhaps because the gesture of the fine gentleman bowing before the donkey is too bizarre and extravagant, and because 'l'esprit de la France' is too vague and general as a concept, 'Un plaisant' remains an anecdote, and we are uncomfortably aware of the poet striving to graft on to this 'accident de sa flânerie' a disagreeable message, which does not manage to rise much above the snide or gratuitously cynical remark.[4]

The impact of a piece such as 'Le Désespoir de la vieille', which relates the despair of an old woman who smilingly approaches a baby and is rebuffed by vigorous infant squallings, may at first seem exceedingly meagre and banal, until we glimpse behind it the literary or cultural commonplace which it upsets. It is a banality to link infancy to old age,[5] and the poem obediently shows us the old woman and the infant, defenceless and frail, without teeth and without hair. There is in the commonplace a sense of recurrence which is not without comfort, a sense of a return not only to innocence when the aged have been removed from action, but also perhaps a sense of a return to origins and a circular view of time in which there is a suggestion of the identity of beginning and end. It is this veiled presence of a cultural commonplace together with the strongly visual properties of the piece which no doubt prompted René Jasinski to describe it as a 'scène familière, qui confine au tableau de genre',[6] and it could well be this also which caused the organizers of the Baudelaire exhibition at the Bibliothèque Nationale in 1957—unconvincingly according to Kopp[7]—to state that the Daumier drawing 'La Vieille Femme et l'enfant' was 'en rapport' with Baudelaire's prose poem. But the organizers were right, only it is a relationship of contrast rather than similarity, since Daumier's drawing shows a serene old woman looking thoughtfully into the face of a placid baby. Baudelaire panders to the *poncif* in the first part of the poem, whose force and 'rayonnement' stem from the sudden 'soubresaut' caused in the mind of the reader who is expecting a reassuring moral message, but is left with a 'morale désagréable' and a poignant sense of solitude and despair.

Commonplaces, platitudes, and 'idées reçues', which fascinated Baudelaire every bit as much as Flaubert, abound in the prose poems, where they serve the purpose of pointing an unpleasant moral lesson in a wilfully prosaic and debilitated style. Superficially and taken out of context, nothing could appear more pedestrian than such statements as 'le crépuscule excite les fous', 'il ne faut pas manger tout son bien en un jour', 'il y a si peu d'amusements qui ne soient pas coupables', 'la pensée est incommunicable'.[8] At first glance, they appear to have the same deflating and prosaic effect as when the poet reminds us in 'Le Chien et le flacon', with the studied uncertainty of the man of taste who wishes to appear ignorant of such lowly matters, that the wagging of a dog's tail is a sign corresponding to smiling or laughing in human beings. But the function of such platitudes is sometimes more complex than may at first appear. For example, the irony of 'il ne faut pas manger tout son bien en un jour' in 'La Femme sauvage et la petite-maîtresse' springs not just from the discrepancy between the mock reasonableness of the husband and the frenzied appetite of the savage wife devouring live rabbits and chickens; it points rather to a total rift between the accepted wisdom of conventional morality and the realities of human nature and passion which they are not able to modify or control. It uncovers the savagery which hides behind the front of decency and reasonableness, with the implication that civilized behaviour is nothing more than controlled rapacity.

On other occasions Baudelaire shows his impatience and distaste for the kind of platitudes which stem from a lax, superficial and sentimental humanitarianism. In 'Les Yeux des pauvres', for example, he ironically quotes the platitude, put forward by such excellent moralists as the writers of popular songs, affirming that 'le plaisir rend l'âme bonne et amollit le cœur',[9] which goes blatantly counter to the events of the anecdote and, of course, to Baudelaire's own view of the corrupting power of pleasure. The irony is clear, since the poet's mistress, far from being moved by the sight of the poor man and his children staring at them as they enjoy the pleasure of the brightly lit new café, finds them insufferable and asks that they be sent away. But even so, the reader cannot find refuge or solace in a sceptical view of human nature, for the irony extends to the poet himself, who confesses that his heart has been moved; he has been 'attendri par cette famille d'yeux', an expression which indicates at one and the same time concern for the poor, an embarrassed self-consciousness, and a humorous detachment which appears to deny the sympathetic *élan*. Though he is ashamed 'de nos verres et de nos carafes, plus grands que notre soif', his attitude towards the family of eyes remains ambivalent; he sympathizes with their feeling of exclusion and is moved by the wonder of the youngest, whose eyes were 'trop fascinés pour exprimer autre chose qu'une joie stupide et profonde', and yet, at the same time, he is aware of the vulgarity of the place, the décor of which, with its Hebes and Ganymedes, expresses 'toute l'histoire et toute la mythologie mises au service de la goinfrerie'. His attitude is, to say the least, complex, being composed of irritation with his mistress, distaste for his surroundings, pity for the poor, which in turn is mingled with embarrassment and the aristocratic aloofness of the dandy who is aware that all men, even the poor, belong to fallen humanity, and are equally likely to be corrupted by pleasure. Towards the end of the poem the poet turns his gaze towards his mistress in the hope of seeing his thoughts reflected in her eyes, but with typical imperturbability she asks him to get the waiter to move the man and his children away, and the poet concludes with the grating cliché: 'Tant il est difficile de s'entendre, mon cher ange, et tant la pensée est incommunicable, même entre gens qui s'aiment'. Without the ironic repetition of 'tant' and the reference to his exasperating mistress as 'mon cher ange', the sentence is the kind of unadorned 'idée reçue' which the poet's mistress would appreciate and possibly utter in moments of feeling misunderstood. But irony is apparent also, since the platitude is raised to the dignity of an article of faith—at least implicitly—by those very people who are so lacking in awareness as to be insensitive to the thoughts, needs, and feelings of other people, by those, in short, who have never made a sustained effort to communicate with other people and who, through lack of imagination, are unable to get out of themselves. The 'idée reçue' belongs to the collective wisdom of those who have never thought beyond themselves and whose unassailable self-sufficiency has shielded them from the real problems of being a human being and, above all, from the awareness of that fundamental void which constitutes our inner loneliness.

At the same time the platitude is appropriated by the poet who has lived out these realities to the full and has sought in vain the Romantic ideal of a spiritual union with the loved one, and whose idealism, like that of Constant's Adolphe or of Nerval, has been misdirected into the fatal and pathetic confusion of love and religion, seen as the ultimate resolution of the contradictions and divisions which beset human beings.

In the light of this, the attitude of the poet towards the poor becomes clear. Just as he has misdirected his idealism into love, erroneously seeing mystery and the promise of happiness in her eyes, 'habités par le Caprice et inspirés par la Lune', so also have the poor mistaken the ostentatious vulgarity of the palace of gluttony as a manifestation of beauty.[10] Both are mistaken, and both are outcasts. In the poor the poet sees a mirror image of himself, but with his illusions still intact; hence the ambivalence of his attitude, made of both sympathy and impatience, endowing the poem with the same moral uncertainty as we find in 'Une mort héroïque' and 'Le Mauvais Vitrier'.

However, there are statements of truth which are even more discreet and whose irony is so delicate as to have a similar effect to the one intended by Flaubert, that the reader does not know 'si on se fout de lui, oui ou non'.[11] For example, the opening sentence of 'Le Joujou du pauvre' might, on first reading, appear perfectly innocent and banal: 'Je veux donner l'idée d'un divertissement innocent. Il y a si peu d'amusements qui ne soient pas coupables!' An uninitiated reader coming upon the piece for the first time in an anthology, or separated from the rest of Baudelaire's work, might well take the statement about amusements at face value and expect to be told of some harmless pastime by some middle-aged author with a benignly tolerant view of human nature. But the reader who has been alerted to Baudelaire's Jansenistic view of the passions, and who has picked up a remote resonance from Pascal's famous passage on 'divertissement', will immediately recognize the irony concealed in the exclamation mark and in the falsely regretful intensifying 'si peu d'amusements'. The author, and his reader, seem to sigh as if dismissing with resignation and regret another little temptation to which they would gladly have given in.

But clearly the full irony of these sentences can only emerge when we learn the true nature of the innocent diversion which takes the form of an experiment. The reader is invited to fill his pockets, before going out to idle in the streets, with all sorts of 'petites inventions à un sol' and to distribute them to the poor children who cross his way. Nothing could appear more innocent; indeed, the action appears charitable, since the children, all agog, are unable to believe in their good fortune. But then we are told that they snatch at the present and run away 'comme font les chats qui vont manger loin de vous le morceau que vous leur avez donné, ayant appris à se défier de l'homme'. The violence of the gesture, the furtive flight away from any companions to play with the toy in solitude as an animal will eat its prey, all point to a natural, spontaneous, primitive animality in children, closer to fallen nature than to redeemed humanity. By concentrating on the scene with the rat, dwelling on the idea of the innocent 'divertissement', and by omitting the long introduction to the much earlier *Morale du joujou* on which the prose poem is based and which deals with the way toys reflect and develop the child's innate aesthetic sense, Baudelaire has, as Zimmerman has suggested,[12] made the two pieces irreconcilable, and instead of a 'morale agréable' which would see children in a favourable light, he has drawn an unpleasant moral which emphasizes their animality and their greater proximity to original sin.

In the light of all this, what are we to make of the innocent pastime? What innocence can there be in an experiment which rejoices in revealing the baseness and animality of mankind? It reveals the guilty nature of man, from which the poet-narrator is not immune, since he provokes such reactions, and rejoices and finds pleasure in the spectacle of evil. The innocent pastime is, in fact, as guilty as the mad cackle of the villain in melodrama which Baudelaire mentions in De l'essence du rire,[13] since it measures the distance that man has fallen from perfection.

Similarly, one suspects that there is more than a little pulling of the reader's leg in the words whispered in the disturbing 'Assommons les pauvres!' by the poet's demon of action who bears some resemblance to the imp of the perverse and to the 'démons malicieux' of 'Le Mauvais Vitrier'. 'Celui-là seul est l'égal d'un autre, qui le prouve, et celui-là seul est digne de la liberté, qui sait la conquérir' appears less as some kind of liberating maxim, which some commentators have suggested, than as a political doctrine reduced to the status of an 'idée reçue' and endowed with the punch and the brutality of a slogan. One would need to subscribe to the social and economic views of the self-made man or to believe that Baudelaire was some kind of precursor of Nietzsche[14] not to suspect some trace of irony in the passage, though it is true that the anarchist Camille Pissarro appears to have taken it uncritically when he used it as an epigraph to his drawing 'Le Mendiant' in Turpitudes sociales. The beggar is seen holding out his hat for alms, his back turned to a shop window stocked with rich food: which prompts the comment from Pissarro in a letter: 'ce parias [sic] n'a pas l'énergie de prendre de force les plantureuses victuailles exposées a [sic] la vitrine derrière lui, il aime mieux mourrir [sic] de faim! étrange!!' Pissarro seems, like some other commentators since, to have fallen into the trap of taking seriously the injunction to beat up the poor to increase their self-reliance, instead of interpreting the piece, like 'Le Reniement de saint Pierre', as an ironical denunciation of the inhumanity of modern society, in which only the strongest and most fortunate can survive, and where it is futile to expect charity. It may well be that, in spite of his view that Proudhon was merely 'un *bon bougre*'[16] and not a dandy, Baudelaire continued to be marked by his social views right down to the time of writing 'Assommons les pauvres!' and that Proudhon's 'mutualisme' is the hidden intertext behind the suppressed last sentence of the manuscript of the poem, 'Qu'en dis-tu, Citoyen Proudhon?'; but from there it is a long way to go to claim, as Dolf Oehler does, that the poem should be read as an incitement to class struggle and revolutionary violence. As Wolfgang Drost says, 'The irony which to such a high degree pervades "Assommons les pauvres!" gives a key to his attitude towards Revolution, an attitude which is one of considerable detachment.'[17] Whatever the exact nature of Baudelaire's political views in 1848 and 1866, I'd suggest that the poem can no more be read as a plea for violence than 'Le Reniement de saint Pierre' can be said to show his scorn for those for whom 'l'action n'est pas la sœur du rêve'.[18] Interpretations of these poems which do not take sufficient account of the poet's irony and his desire to mystify run the grave risk of being naïvely literal. The convulsive violence of the piece, and the picture of the beggar holding out his hat for alms 'avec un de ces regards inoubliables qui culbuteraient les trônes, si l'esprit remuait la matière', like that of Christ 'monté sur une douce ânesse', seem to indicate that the key to both pieces should be found not 'dans l'intertexte de Proudhon', but in a veiled and ironic reference to that part of the Sermon on the Mount which proclaims the blessedness of the meek, 'for they shall inherit the earth'.

Baudelaire's use of the popular saying is clearly linked to his preoccupation with the commonplace and the 'idée reçue'. Sometimes the saying is merely incidental, its function being simply to produce a clash of linguistic register, as, for example, with 'chercher midi à quatorze heures' in 'La Fausse Monnaie'. Sometimes the saying lies hidden below the surface of the text, as with 'la corde du pendu' in 'La Corde' and 'les auréoles changent souvent de tête' in 'Perte d'auréole'; and at other times Baudelaire will revitalize expressions such as 'la vie en beau', 'marchand de nuages', and 'tuer le temps', in order to give an insight into the complex situation of the poet and his relationship to his art, showing his ability to exploit the secret depths, the 'profondeur immense de pensée dans les locutions vulgaires, trous creusés par des générations de fourmis'.[19] Even as early as in 1857 in 'L'Invitation au voyage', a more conventionally 'lyrical'

poem in which Baudelaire still seems uncertain about what he wished
to achieve in the genre,[20] the popular saying or expression has a role
to play, its function in the exclamation 'Moi, j'ai trouvé ma *tulipe
noire et mon dahlia bleu!*' being able to provide an ironic 'soubresaut'
by juxtaposing the researches of the alchemists of horticulture and
the poet's discovery of the geographical counterpart to the soul of
his mistress, with the result that the reader hesitates in his interpretation and reaction between dignifying the search for an unusual
flower and degrading the spiritual quest of the poet. Is the poet's
dream of the perfect correspondence between his mistress and an
ideal country as gratuitous and trivial as the search for an unnatural
tulip or dahlia, or can the search for the unnatural flower be seen
as another manifestation of man's search for the impossible, a
spiritual quest revealing the superiority of the mind and of art over
nature? It is no doubt because it provides him with such fruitful
ambiguities that Baudelaire finds 'rien de plus beau que le lieu
commun'[21] and that he uses it with increasing frequency in the prose
poems of the sixties.

   In 'Le Tir et le cimetière' he plays with the popular expression
'mettre dans le but', giving it a double meaning, both to hit the
mark and die, by alluding to the dead as those who 'depuis longtemps
ont mis dans le But, dans le seul vrai but de la détestable vie'.
Zimmerman[22] has suggested a parallel between the prose poem and
'La Mort des artistes' whose first quatrain reads as follows:

> Combien faut-il de fois secouer mes grelots
> Et baiser ton front bas, morne caricature?
> Pour piquer dans le but, de mystique nature,
> Combien, ô mon carquois, perdre de javelots?

But the 'but' of the sonnet is the elusive image of poetic beauty and
the figure is dignified by the comparison of the poet to a hunter with
his bow and arrows, with the result that any sense of a discrepancy
between tenor and vehicle, and any consequent dissonance, is rapidly
muted; whereas in the prose poem the effect of the figure is doubly
discordant because of the macabrely comic intrusion of a popular
expression into the prosopopeia of the dead ('Maudites soient vos
cibles [. . .] Maudites soient vos ambitions, maudits soient vos
calculs', etc.), and the grim appropriateness of human beings
practising shooting and the art of killing beside the sanctuary of
death (cf. 'Un cabaret folâtre'). Furthermore, the play upon words

operates a curious reversal of the figure, and with it a whole associated vocabulary which deals with men's aims and the achievement of their ends of happiness and freedom—so that 'mettre dans le But' ceases to mean to practise the art of shooting or achieving one's ambitions, but rather to aim at killing oneself, to bring about one's own death as the only aim in life. The idea that death ends everything and is the only meaning of life is a banality;[23] but the idea, stemming from the renovation of the figure, that death is the sole purpose of life which all men are enthusiastically pursuing even when they think themselves free and defending or enhancing their lives, reaches greater depths of originality and gloom. And indeed the figure seems to carry further, moral and social, overtones with the implication that by shooting at the range and by studying the art of killing the activities of men involve a positive hostility towards others, so that the negative image of the human condition is doubled by an equally negative image of society.

'Chacun sa chimère' has the overtones and the form of a proverb or popular saying such as 'chacun son goût', or 'chacun son beau'. It also has something of the captions which great caricaturists like Daumier or Goya used for their drawings, and indeed it has been very convincingly suggested that in writing this piece Baudelaire had in mind the *capricho* by Goya entitled 'Tu que no puedes', which depicts Spaniards carrying on their backs asses with faintly human expressions. As Jean Prévost has pointed out, the moral message is clear and simple: Spain is groaning under the oppression of fools. Prévost is also right to say that in this poem Baudelaire 'entrevoit devant ce dessin une vérité humaine et immense: chacun de nous porte sa Chimère, sans même la voir',[24] though it is a pity that his analysis of the figure stops at this point. Baudelaire's insight implies that men are totally in the grip of a huge 'chimère' of which they know nothing and which drives them along independently of their will. Whereas Vigny's poem 'Les Destinées', to which 'Chacun sa chimère' has been compared, sees men in the grip of fate and of predestination,[25] Baudelaire makes of the chimera something resembling the dictates of the unconscious mind. Furthermore, it is clear that there is nowhere to go in this bleak and desolate landscape which has been compared to Dante's limbo,[26] and that there can be no possible realization of the vain ideals which push men along and give unfailing hope to those who have 'la physionomie résignée de ceux qui sont condamnés à espérer toujours'. Baudelaire's view of mankind in this prose poem is similar to Beckett's in *Waiting for Godot* or to Gisors's in *La Condition humaine*, where it is stated that 'sans doute, au plus profond, Gisors était-il espoir comme il était angoisse, espoir de rien, attente'.[27] The moral of the piece is made even more melancholy in the final paragraph in which the poet seeks in vain to understand the mystery of this nightmarish vision, but stops short, overwhelmed by indifference which weighs on him even more heavily than the 'Chimères' on their victims. The moral is more pessimistic and unpleasant than in 'L'Invitation au voyage' where it is proclaimed triumphantly and with only the merest suspicion of irony that 'chaque homme porte en lui sa dose d'opium naturel'; men are deluded and their lives are dictated by chimeras which give them hope in a hopeless world; without such illusions and false hope, man is perhaps free, but it is a freedom to do and to believe in nothing.

Baudelaire's use of the expression 'tuer le temps' in 'Le Galant Tireur' has been very ingeniously, and somewhat punningly, analysed by Barbara Johnson[28] in order, primarily, to show the mechanics of figural language. I should like to add some comments which might help to elucidate the poem within the specific context of the poet's preoccupation with a 'morale désagréable'. It would be useful to quote the whole of the poem.

Comme la voiture traversait le bois, il la fit arrêter dans le voisinage d'un tir, disant qu'il lui serait agréable de tirer quelques balles pour *tuer* le Temps. Tuer ce monstre-là, n'est-ce pas l'occupation la plus ordinaire et la plus légitime de chacun? — Et il offrit galamment la main à sa chère, délicieuse et exécrable femme, à cette mystérieuse femme à laquelle il doit tant de plaisirs, tant de douleurs, et peut-être aussi une grande partie de son génie.

Plusieurs balles frappèrent loin du but proposé; l'une d'elles s'enfonça même dans le plafond; et comme la charmante créature riait follement, se moquant de la maladresse de son époux, celui-ci se tourna brusquement vers elle, et lui dit: 'Observez cette poupée, là-bas, à droite, qui porte le nez en l'air et qui a la mine si hautaine. Eh bien! cher ange, *je me figure que c'est vous.*' Et il ferma les yeux et il lâcha la détente. La poupée fut nettement décapitée.

Alors s'inclinant vers sa chère, sa délicieuse, son exécrable femme, son inévitable et impitoyable Muse, et lui baisant respectueusement la main, il ajouta: 'Ah! mon cher ange, combien je vous remercie de mon adresse!'

As Barbara Johnson says, the two figures of killing Time and decapitating the doll are closely related. In everyday existence one kills time in order to escape from boredom and, as the poem wryly indicates, what could be more natural or legitimate? But Baudelaire italicizes *kill* and capitalizes Time to renovate and resuscitate a dead metaphor which has itself been killed by time and usage (Johnson), and to indicate also that the desire to kill time stems not so much from the common boredom which affects all men and which is no doubt the principal *raison d'être* of firing ranges, but from the apprehension that time is the enemy of man, that it is the stuff of our imperfection, making it impossible for us ever to achieve that god-like completion and unity of being to which we aspire, and perpetually reminding us that our state is one of dispersion, fragmentation, and becoming. To kill Time we would need more than a firing range, we would need a fundamental transformation of the relationship of consciousness with the world resulting in the impossible synthesis of 'en-soi' and 'pour-soi' which Sartre speculates on in *L'Être et le néant*; but the figure is appropriate because the violence involved in the anecdote hints at a kind of paroxysm of frustration as the bullets are fired 'loin du but proposé'. The implication would seem to be that, though he cannot kill time with a capital T, for his wife, who cannot understand his intentions and who finds his antics amusing, time with a small t is effectively killed. At this point the poet substitutes mentally his wife for the doll and there ensues a ritual killing in effigy which gives an extremely macabre tone to what was at first an innocent firing range. The killing in effigy exemplifies the relationship between love and violence which Baudelaire treats elsewhere in 'Mademoiselle Bistouri', 'Les Tentations', and 'A celle qui est trop gaie', and critics[29] have suggested convincingly that there may be a link between 'Le Galant Tireur' and the anecdote of the hunter in *Journaux intimes* dealing with the 'liaison intime de la férocité et de l'amour'.[30] But more than that, the shooting in effigy points to the problematical relationship between the poet and art, symbolized by his wife as muse. She is both execrable and delightful. He owes to her a great deal of his genius, not so much because she elevates his thoughts towards higher things, but because the discrepancy between her physical attractions, and the accompanying associations which they give rise to, and her spiritual and intellectual nullity so irritates him that, shutting his eyes as if inspired, he aims correctly and decapitates the doll. This bitter little piece can be seen as a symbol of artistic creation in which the poet's muse inspires him to perfection, but only through a ritual whereby he imagines he is killing the very thing which inspires him. The opposites of creation and destruction are overcome in an ironic paradox in which the poet's spurious romantic angel causes a kind of 'salut à rebours' by projecting him into a hell of incompatibility, irritation, and violence. The bullet hits its mark, and at the same time the imperfections of the muse are transformed in the perfection of the poet's skill. The moral lesson is doubly paradoxical; the conscious attempt to kill Time is a vain frenzy, and what would a poet do without a muse to inspire him but fall a prey to Time and ennui which cannot be killed? But to kill the wife-muse fictitiously is to accede to the 'ivresse de l'art' which at least momentarily gives the illusion of having killed Time and, at the same time, renders the muse's imperfection an instrument of artistic perfection.

The poem is clearly closely linked to 'Portraits de maîtresses' by the use of the expression 'tuer le temps', by the killing (this time real) of the mistress, and by the contradictions in the notion of perfection. The poem involves the reminiscences of four middle-aged dandies of the extraordinary mistresses they had known. The most bizarre and interesting story is that of the fourth dandy who tells how he had to get rid of his mistress for the paradoxical reason that she was perfect; 'incapable de commettre une erreur de sentiment ou de calcul', she had 'une sérénité désolante de caractère; un dévouement sans comédie et sans emphase; une douceur sans faiblesse; une énergie sans violence'. With a cold and invincible will, she had barred the way to all his caprices, so that in his frustration he admired her with a heart full of hatred, in the end drowning her one evening in a pond in a lonely wood. The story momentarily intrigues and surprises the cynical companions until, at last, new bottles are brought and they resume their drinking 'pour tuer le Temps qui a la vie si dure, et accélérer la Vie qui coule si lentement'. The contrasts between the dead-pan narration of the remorseless drowning (euphemistically referred to as 'une action rigoureuse') and their normal drinking habits, and secondly, between the ease with which she is disposed of as if by magic and the 'grands moyens' of alcoholic poisoning which have to be used to kill the much more resilient Time, are, of course, highly amusing and ironic, and there is something positively grating and sick in the use of the popular saying within the context of a real killing which is accepted so readily. The saying maintains its triteness which is pushed to the point of vulgarity and bad taste, and at the same time the reader, shocked at the author's evident 'plaisir aristocratique de déplaire',[31] is aware of its many wider resonances and subtleties. As in 'Le Galant Tireur' the popular saying

is revitalized, with the result that a real killing replaces the meta-
phorical killing of time in order precisely to kill Time and deliver
from ennui; for, as Robert Kopp says in his edition,[32] 'la raison de
l'assassinat disparaît, elle devient métaphysique', since it is based
upon the absolute incompatibility between moral beauty and life,
or, as Baudelaire himself puts it in the *Salon* of 1846: 'Les poètes,
les artistes et toute la race humaine seraient bien malheureux, si
l'idéal, cette absurdité, cette impossibilité, était trouvé. Qu'est-ce
que chacun ferait désormais de son pauvre *moi*, — de sa ligne
brisée?'[33] The moral of the two pieces taken together is that we need
imperfection in order to aspire towards a perfection which will
remain perfect provided it is never realized. In their contrasting and
opposite ways the two stories go to the heart of Baudelaire's aesthetics
and, implicitly, of his strangely incomplete and agnostic Christianity,
since they depict men with aspirations to which nothing in this world
can correspond and which nothing can fulfil.

Baudelaire's use of the aphorism and of the moral maxim is even
more subtle and complex than his use of the commonplace and
popular saying. He seems to have been intrigued by the possibilities
of the genre from a very early stage in his career, and a brief survey
of his practice in other writings would help to elucidate its various
functions in the prose poems. The *Choix de maximes consolantes
sur l'amour*, which he sent as a rather cruel joke to the bewildered and
prudish wife of his half-brother Alphonse, is a useful starting-point.
Its opening sentence, 'Quiconque écrit des maximes aime charger
son caractère; — les jeunes se griment, — les vieux s'adonisent',[34]
provides, assuredly, an arresting 'entrée en matière', not so much
for its pithiness or sententiousness, as for its manifest unreliability.
A maxim which calls in question the motives of creators of maxims
(who, according to a more orthodox view, might be thought to have
a greater degree of self-knowledge than most men), does not attract
immediate confidence and belief, having something of the self-
defeating qualities of the notice which states that 'all notices on this
board are false'. The reader is left wondering whether such a maxim
has not itself been contaminated by the inauthenticity of its progenitor
which it unashamedly proclaims, so that the maxim and the ensuing
piece it presides over appear, as they were no doubt intended to,
as a kind of 'spoof' designed to amuse, and possibly to mystify, the

reader by a display of literary pyrotechnics. The undisguised pastiche of Stendhal's *De l'amour*, and, above all, the flippant and ironic tone evident in the inflated sententiousness of the 'maximes particulières sur des questions délicates' and in the 'patois séminariste', dealing with the problem of freedom in theology and in love, enable the young Baudelaire, as in *La Fanfarlo*, to put forward some of his principal ideas concerning physiognomy, Nature, the union of opposites, moral and physical beauty and ugliness in women, and to detach himself at the same time and take no responsibility for them. Nathaniel Wing's very pertinent remarks on *La Fanfarlo*[35] are also relevant to the *Choix de maximes*; for what is at issue is style as well as thematic substance, the somewhat oblique criticism falling not just upon a certain Romantic bric-à-brac, but on Romantic rhetoric as well. Consequently, the sententious utterances of the piece appear both as commonplaces which are to be condemned for their banality, and as truths rendered problematic by the self-conscious posturing of a young writer both claiming and rejecting, in default of a style of his own, a wisdom beyond the reach, and possibly even the conviction, of his years.

At the opposite pole to this decidedly ambivalent attitude, and as evidence of the poet's enduring preoccupation with binary opposites, we find in the section of the *Journaux intimes* entitled 'Hygiène' the grave injunctions and moral principles which he strives to adopt in order to improve the conduct of his life[36] and to make it more purposeful and creative: 'Plus on travaille, mieux on travaille, et plus on veut travailler. Plus on produit, plus on devient fécond.'[37] Or take the following rule which is also a 'cri du cœur': 'Faire tous les matins ma *prière à Dieu, réservoir de toute force et de toute justice*, à *mon père*, à *Mariette* et à *Poe*, comme intercesseurs'.[38] This belief in the almost magical power of prayer is also present in a maxim which, were it not for the poignant circumstances, might be thought to be invalidated by the solemnity and the unsophistication of a 'bon sentiment', unworthy of the great poet: 'L'homme qui fait sa prière le soir est un capitaine qui pose des sentinelles. Il peut dormir.'[39] His aim in these private notations is to establish a 'sagesse abrégée' based on the triple foundation of 'Toilette, prière, travail',[40] in order to correct the anarchy of his life and to pinpoint some uncertainties in the midst of doubt and chaos. It is ironic that in striving for regeneration he should use the same turn of phrase as he used, damningly, to praise the moral and psychological over-simplifications of Hugo whom he pictured 'appuyé sur une sagesse abrégée, faite de quelques axiomes irréfutables',[41] in much the same way as the characters of *Les Misérables* were to appear to him all of a piece, reduced to one or two invariable character traits. However, the flippancy of the 'maximes consolantes', which seem to indicate some doubts about the validity of writing maxims, and the simple moral injunctions of 'Hygiène' did not prevent Baudelaire from taking the genre seriously and from being an excellent practitioner of it, as other parts of the *Journaux intimes* testify. But what is not altogether clear is the status of the various maxims and sentences in the *Journaux*. It is most likely that the ones we find in 'Mon Cœur mis à nu' would have lost much of their sententiousness and their fragmentary appearance within the elaboration of the autobiography itself, in much the same way as Pascal's *Pensées* would have been transformed in the completed apology. The famous 'De la vaporisation et de la centralisation du *Moi*. Tout est là.'[42] (is it a maxim or merely a note?) might well have lost some of its mystery, which has prompted so much ingenious interpretation, once inserted into a particular context, biographical, psychological, aesthetic, or moral. And what are we to make of the 'fusée' enigmatically couched in the form of a question: 'Se livrer à Satan, qu'est-ce que c'est?'[43] Would Baudelaire have published it along with other similar mind-expanding utterances and maxims, would it have become part of a chapter on his own life and his view of the senses, or would it have become an exploration of the moral and theological meaninglessness of the notion of giving oneself knowingly to the Devil? Whatever the many possible answers to such speculations may be, what is clear is the wide variety of the genre to be found in the *Journaux* and the section entitled 'Aphorismes' in the two-volume Pléiade *Œuvres complètes*. They range from the highly serious utterances on psychology, aesthetics, and theology to such frivolous 'boutades' as 'Si un poète demandait à l'État le droit d'avoir quelques bourgeois dans son écurie, on serait fort étonné, tandis que si un bourgeois demandait du poète rôti, on le trouverait tout naturel.'[44] The humour arises here not least from the incongruity of the perfect balance of the form and the triviality of the content. One can find strident vulgarities about women alongside bizarre definitions such as the one recorded in Asselineau's *carnet* to the effect that 'Un chat est un vampire sucré',[45] enhanced in surreality by the alternative reading 'vampire sacré', which seems to forbid one to speculate in public about the kind of fantasy which can produce such exquisitely decadent thoughts about the domestic cat.

However, it is in *Le Spleen de Paris* that we find the highest incidence of maxims and commonplaces in Baudelaire's works— predictably, at least at first sight, since such utterances would appear to belong primarily to the domain of prose and to be out of place in lyric poetry; and indeed, if we discount such metaphors as 'La Haine est un ivrogne au fond d'une taverne' in 'Le Tonneau de la Haine', *Les Fleurs du Mal* provides few examples of sententiousness. Some of the prose poems amalgamate and elaborate notations from the *Journaux intimes*. For example, the famous comments on love, religion, art, and prostitution—'L'amour, c'est le goût de la prostitution. [. . .] Qu'est-ce que l'art? Prostitution.'[46] 'L'être le plus prostitué, c'est l'être par excellence, c'est Dieu'[47]—are fused and developed in 'Les Foules', culminating in the splendid 'fusée' and article of faith: 'Ce que les hommes nomment amour est bien petit, bien restreint et bien faible, comparé à cette ineffable orgie, à cette sainte prostitution de l'âme qui se donne tout entière, poésie et charité, à l'imprévu qui se montre, à l'inconnu qui passe.' And the bizarre comparison of love to surgery, 'Il y a dans l'acte de l'amour une grande ressemblance avec la torture, ou avec une opération chirurgicale',[48] which is suggested in 'Les Tentations', where Eros appears with sinister phials and surgical instruments hanging from the snake which serves as a living belt round his middle, is exemplified and dramatized in 'Mademoiselle Bistouri', which also takes up the theme of prostitution. The sententiousness disappears in the anecdote, which sets the abstractions of the maxim in a real person and a real place. And this concretization of an arresting though somewhat cryptic maxim, paradoxically, has the effect of an increase of suggestiveness, as the reader is led to reflect not just on the sado-masochistic elements already present in the original sentence and the reversal of the usual associations of love with pleasure and tenderness, but on the implication that the paradox of love, involving, as it would seem, both tenderness and cruelty, could not be lived out by any sane person, and that sensuality and intellect must be totally dissociated before one can enter what Proust called 'le monde inhumain du plaisir',[49] that domain of the perverse or of the 'monstres innocents' who are out of their minds.

Baudelaire's interest in the great 'moralistes' of the past is witnessed in the frequent mention in his works and correspondence of Bossuet,

Buffon, Chamfort, Fénelon, Joubert, La Bruyère, La Fontaine, Pascal, and Vauvenargues; but it is significant that it is in the prose poems that he makes the most specific references and quotes, or rather misquotes, them. Buffon has a glancing reference in 'Les Bons Chiens', Vauvenargues's 'Sur les misères cachées' is present in the introduction to 'Les Veuves', and La Bruyère and Pascal figure directly in 'La Solitude', whose first sentence, 'Un gazetier philanthrope me dit que la solitude est mauvaise pour l'homme', contains, possibly, a muffled echo of le père Souël's words at the end of René : 'La solitude est mauvaise à celui qui n'y vit pas avec Dieu.'⁵⁰ Such references have, no doubt, the familiar function of giving authority to the speculations of a learned, but still relatively unknown, writer, and the misquotations from La Bruyère and Pascal could be explained by a desire for concision and terseness within the necessary economy of the 'petit poème en prose', though it should be noted that Baudelaire took the misquotation from La Bruyère from Poe's *The Man of the Crowd*. But one wonders why he should add to the misquotation of the passage in the *Pensées* concerning man's inability to remain within the four walls of his room 'dit un autre sage, Pascal, je crois', and how to interpret the patronizing and falsely uncertain attribution of what is, after all, one of Pascal's most famous thoughts, a commonplace recognizable by any schoolboy; unless Baudelaire wishes both to embrace and to play down the wisdom of the great man and, in a collection which praises the virtues of both solitude and of the 'bain de multitude', to cast doubt upon the validity of such acknowledged truths which, before the complexities of real life, appear as glib and facile as an 'idée reçue'.⁵²

Such uncertainties are of course deliberate and intended to mystify the reader, or at least some readers. One of the most interesting examples is 'La Corde', where the narrator remains deluded even at the end of his narration, which is supposed to record the circumstances in which he lost his illusions. In this highly complex and bitter piece Baudelaire's comment about the makers of maxims in the *Choix de maximes...* seems very appropriate; for the narrator's recourse to such resounding truths as 'Les illusions sont aussi innombrables peut-être que les rapports des hommes entre eux', 'Il est aussi difficile de supposer une mère sans amour maternel qu'une lumière sans chaleur', and 'Les douleurs les plus terribles sont les douleurs muettes', is accompanied by a pomposity of tone betraying a desire to 'se grimer' and to appear full of experience and sagacity. Many critics have

followed the narrator in the belief that the story shows that even
so fundamental an instinct as maternal love can be corrupted by the
love of money, and nothing more. But such an interpretation smacks
of the 'idée reçue' and is, in any case, as we have seen in Chapter I,
rendered suspect by the narrator's self-satisfaction, glibness, and
insensitivity to the real needs and feelings of the boy, whom he treats
more as an object than as a human being. It is Baudelaire's skilful
use of maxims and commonplaces which helps to direct the reader's
attention away from the superficial meaning of the poem about the
nature of mother love towards its deeper implications about the
nature and validity of art itself.

The prose poems abound in maxims of Baudelaire's own coining
which would not have disgraced his great predecessors in the
seventeenth and eighteenth centuries. Among his greatest 'trouvailles'
are what I should like to call his 'aphorismes-abîmes' which either
introduce or conclude a poem, and form its substance. I am thinking
of such statements as 'L'étude du beau est un duel où l'artiste crie
de frayeur avant d'être vaincu', the one concerning 'sainte prostitution',
or 'Cette vie est un hôpital où chaque malade est possédé du désir
de changer de lit'. Such aphorisms contain a great depth of philo-
sophical, artistic, or moral truth and have the power to impress
themselves on the memory and fascinate the mind with their many
ramifications. Take, for example, the statement which concludes and
sums up 'La Fausse Monnaie': 'le plus irréparable des vices est de
faire le mal par bêtise'. The anecdote concerns a friend of the poet
who astonishes a grateful beggar by the generous gift of a coin of
unexpected value. But the coin is false and the poet eventually
understands that his friend 'avait voulu faire à la fois la charité et
une bonne affaire; gagner quarante sols et le cœur de Dieu; emporter
le paradis économiquement; enfin attraper gratis un brevet d'homme
charitable', and the poet concludes the piece with the statement that
the most irreparable of vices is to do evil out of stupidity. At first
sight the statement might appear to go counter to common sense
which would tend to excuse an evil act if the intention was not evil.
Most people would wish to distinguish subjective from objective
guilt, and would accept that stupidity would be a mitigating factor,
since it involves a degree of innocence and an inability to assess the
evil and its consequences. The anecdote, which has the appearance
of an amusing real experience, gives on to a profound view of human
nature, since the poet's stupid friend appears beyond redemption,

having no awareness or knowledge of his evil. The curse upon Adam and Eve, as they were driven from the garden of Eden, was that they would be like gods knowing good and evil, and this knowledge, as Pascal reminds us, is both our grandeur and our 'misère', since, though it cuts us off from paradise, it gives us the means of a possible salvation, the spiritual life which might bring us back to God. Baudelaire was of course well aware of Pascal's lesson, which no doubt presided over his impatience with the pastoral innocence of George Sand's creations and his admiration for Madame de Merteuil in *Les Liaisons dangereuses*. He was well aware that 'la conscience dans le Mal' is the sign and proof of our humanity. The 'étourderie' of the poet's friend is worse than culpable; it makes of him a sub-man, a curious hybrid creature, a moral and metaphysical accident, deprived at once of the innocence of man before the Fall and of the intelligence which would explain his presence in time and the fallen world, and dignify him as a man. He is a kind of monster at large in a limbo between a paradise he does not know he has lost and a hell which he fails to recognize. The vice is irreparable because unconscious, and Baudelaire's condemnation of the man is final.

It is interesting that the poet should entertain the passing thought that his friend's action might be excused by a desire to see which of many possible outcomes might result from giving to the beggar apparently so large a sum. Would it lead to prison, or to the foundation of a great fortune? Such curiosity would relate the friend to Gide's curious waiter in *Prométhé mal enchaîné* whose fascination with bizarre situations leads him to set at the same table people who appear totally different or incompatible. Spurred on by such an idea, the poet's imagination 'allait son train, prêtant des ailes à l'esprit de mon ami et tirant toutes les déductions possibles de toutes les hypothèses possibles'. It is easy to see how such an idea would explain his friend's action, but it is hard to see how it would justify it. A passage from *L'École païenne* of 1852 which, as Kopp[53] has pointed out, contains the germ of the prose poem, is illuminating in this context:

Le goût immodéré de la forme pousse à des désordres monstrueux et inconnus. Absorbées par la passion féroce du beau, du drôle, du joli, du pittoresque, car il y a des degrés, les notions du juste et du vrai disparaissent. La passion frénétique de l'art est un chancre qui dévore le reste; et, comme l'absence nette du juste et du vrai dans l'art équivaut à l'absence d'art, l'homme entier s'évanouit; la spécialisation excessive d'une faculté aboutit au néant. [. . .] La folie de l'art est égale à l'abus de l'esprit. La création d'une de ces deux suprématies engendre la sottise, la dureté du cœur et une immensité d'orgueil et d'égoïsme. Je me rappelle avoir entendu dire à un artiste farceur qui avait reçu une pièce de monnaie fausse: Je la garde pour un pauvre. Le misérable prenait un infernal plaisir à voler le pauvre et à jouir en même temps des bénéfices d'une réputation de charité.

The passage establishes a parallel between the art for art's sake school and the spurious generosity of the 'artiste farceur'. Just as the art for art's sake writers are forgetful of the notions of justice and truth in their search for what is beautiful, picturesque, or strange, so also is the 'farceur' forgetful of his own basic humanity and that of the poor man. While suppressing the analogy with the artists of the pagan school, Baudelaire in 'La Fausse Monnaie' has kept an element of the original analogy which is its psychological and moral interest. The friend's need for newness and *drôlerie* is put forward as a possible explanation of his conduct, only to be dismissed and replaced by the explanation that he was seeking a cheap way to heaven and that he has committed the act out of sheer stupidity alone. The moral message is thus all the stronger for being undiluted, although one should point out that the poet's attitude towards sententiousness is not without ambiguity, as is evidenced in the way his naïvely proffered 'bon sentiment'—'après le plaisir d'être étonné, il n'en est pas de plus grand que celui de causer une surprise'—is appropriated by his fraudulently generous friend.

The second 'aphorisme-abîme' I should like to discuss is one which is not entirely original. As Margaret Gilman[54] has pointed out, the arresting opening sentence of 'Any where out of this world', 'Cette vie est un hôpital où chaque malade est possédé du désir de changer de lit', appears to have been directly inspired by Emerson's statement in the final chapter of *The Conduct of Life* that 'Like sick men in hospitals, we change only from bed to bed'. Baudelaire's interest in Emerson is well known, and it is generally agreed that we are undoubtedly in the presence here of a more or less certain source. However, there can, I think, be no question of his deliberately misquoting Emerson as he had with La Bruyère and Pascal in order to create an ambiguous tone. Even although the Emerson sentence does not appear in Baudelaire's list from *The Conduct of Life*,[55] it is very unlikely that in the prose poem he was quoting from memory. What he has done is to improve on Emerson's idea and to give it a power and, above all, a universality and a permanence which are absent in the original. Emerson's comparison of our actions to those of sick men in hospitals changing beds appears weak when set against Baudelaire's metaphor in which life is said to be a hospital, thus emphasizing the permanence of the state and increasing the pessimism which informs what has now become a striking maxim.

Once again we find ourselves in presence of a maxim which contains a whole philosophy, an 'aphorisme-abîme'. Nothing could be further from the attitude of some eighteenth-century rationalists who would affirm after Voltaire in one of his more confident moods that 'L'homme paraît être à sa place dans la nature',[56] and that, consequently, there is a kind of 'correspondance' between man's desire for order and rationality and the order of the universe. According to such a view, to affirm that somehow man and the world are not compatible or that they were not 'made' for each other, would be as foolish as to suggest that the fish is not at home in the water. The preoccupation of the Romantics with Plato and certain aspects of Christianity was responsible for the decline, at least among writers, in such a belief, which was replaced by an attitude which emphasized the discrepancy between man and his world and which lived out a sense of a tragic distance between them, which Voltaire certainly knew, but did not choose to celebrate or to magnify.[57] Indeed, for some writers the more a man felt separated not just from society, but from the world, the greater the sense of exile and the greater his superiority. The superior man is not he in whom the faculties work together to produce balance, happiness, and sanity, but rather he whose sense of exile, imbalance, and inner turmoil cause him to embrace madness as opposed to sanity, and alienation and illness as opposed to integration and health. Hence the prestige of the Werthers and Renés, and of the 'femme fatale' and her male counterpart. It is clear that Baudelaire's maxim participates in such a view, but with none of the languid yearning and elegant other-worldliness of René. The illness which is life is no longer the affliction of a spiritual élite, but of all mankind, and the idealism and the elegance have been replaced by a realism which sees life as a hospital in which all mankind, though incurably ill, is possessed of the foolish notion that one might be cured by changing position. And, of course, the figure of a hospital leads the mind to the immediate paradox that the only cure for life is death. The normal associations of life—health, abundance, happiness, fulfilment, hope, renewal—are all illusory. 'Vivre est un mal';[58] life is illness, restriction, imprisonment, stunting, negation, with not even the notion of a window, as in Mallarmé's poem,[59] to give some sense of hope; and the cure lies in extinction.

Baudelaire's often ironic remodelling of the popular saying is such as to deprive it of any reassuring qualities it may have had, and to point to an unstable and chaotic world where there is little in the way of certainty in human values, actions, or motives. Similarly, his own, on occasion, highly original maxims and aphorisms bear witness to his desire to avoid a literature of 'bons sentiments', such as he detested in George Sand and in Victor Hugo's novels; and, like the popular saying, they articulate not stable truths and essences, but the sudden, and often provisional and contradictory illuminations of the 'pensée rapsodique'. Thus, in order to give expression to his 'morale désagréable', he deliberately cultivates paradox and statements which, at first sight at least, go counter to common sense and experience. They often have a palpably refutable quality until the mind of the reader, fascinated by their explosive force, comes to an understanding of a wider and deeper reality. By juxtaposing two contradictory areas of experience, such maxims have a power to inflame the mind in the same way as the most daring and successful similes and metaphors, and they take on some of the dynamite and the brilliance of the 'fusée'.[60] There is something profoundly shocking, causing a violent 'soubresaut de la conscience', in these 'comparaisons énormes'[61] where life is compared to a hospital, and poetic creation to a prostitution which is said to be holy. It is precisely the widening of the gap between tenor and vehicle, and the stridency of the juxtaposition which create an emotional charge which is more violent and jarring than anything produced in *Les Fleurs du Mal*, where, of course, the regular metres and the harmony of rhyme and rhythm domesticate the inherent wildness of some of the images. It was perhaps because of this aspect of Baudelaire's maxims and commonplaces that André Breton thought him 'surréaliste dans la morale'.[62] On the most superficial level, one can interpret their high incidence and wide variety in the prose poems as proof of Baudelaire's desire to mingle the genres and to create a new art form by adding to the 'ondulations de la rêverie' the 'soubresauts' of the most uncompromising prose. But their concision, suggestiveness, irony, paradoxicality, and intellectual radiance which give them the power of the most successful poetic images, together with the number of ideas and reveries[63] they arouse in the mind of the reader bear witness to the fulfilment of his desire to be 'toujours poète, même en prose'.[64]

The moral lesson which Baudelaire draws in the prose poems is predominantly pessimistic, and the world he evokes is one in which order and reason have been replaced by anarchy in both the moral and the physical spheres; for in these poems men are not fundamentally rational creatures; they act without premeditation, or against their own best interests; they light cigars beside barrels of gunpowder to tempt destiny; they boast of unworthy actions they have not committed and refuse to do a small service for a friend, yet they readily help the unworthy; they throw chickens at *maîtres d'hôtel* at the time of the full moon. They fall in love with those with whom they have nothing in common and kill their favourite buffoon or perfect mistress, to such an extent that one would be apt to attribute to Baudelaire the invention of the gratuitous act long before Gide thought of it. It may well be that the function of gratuitous acts in Baudelaire's own life is, as Sartre would have it, a means whereby the dandy tries to 'transformer [. . .] sa vie en destin'[65] and to make himself the victim rather than the perpetrator of events. Such mysteries can be left to the competence of psychoanalysts, since, if one examines the universe which is created in and by the poems themselves, one will see clearly that their function is to show the moral anarchy which lies at the heart of all human actions and emotions. In 'Les Tentations', for example, the poet in his high-mindedness rejects in his dream the blandishments of Eros, Plutus, and Fame, but in his waking life he ironically implores them to return so that he can succumb to them. Similarly, in 'Le Joueur généreux' he rejects the Devil's offer that, in return for his soul, he should be free from ennui; any wish will be granted. But the offer is rejected not out of any strength of mind or character, but out of suspicion, distrust, and an inability to believe in his good fortune; and the poet finds himself praying to God to make the Devil keep his word, a sure sign of moral, spiritual, and theological chaos. Indeed, all the prayers in the collection are, to say the least, unorthodox. In 'A une heure du matin' the poet prays to God to grant him the power to produce some fine verses to prove to himself that he is not inferior to those whom he despises, a prayer which is hardly informed by Christian humility and charity. Indeed, it has more than a trace of the Pharisee's prayer in Luke:[66] 'God, I thank thee, that I am not as other men are, extortioners, unjust, adulterers, or even as this publican'—which is refused in favour of that of the humble and truly repentant publican. It is not at all difficult to accept with Zimmerman[67] that the prayer is not authentic, since there is a contradiction in praying to God for confirmation that one is superior to those one scorns, and Zimmerman goes on to quote Georges Blin's excellent *Le Sadisme de Baudelaire* which he thinks casts light on 'A une heure du matin': 'Ce que Baudelaire souhaite [. . .] c'est un Dieu que l'on puisse prier sans avoir besoin de se sacrifier à lui, et même, à la limite, sans qu'il soit nécessaire de croire en son existence.'[68] However much this statement illuminates Baudelaire's attitude to prayer in general, it does not perhaps fully account for the complexities of this particular instance. It would be useful to quote the prayer in full:

Âmes de ceux que j'ai aimés, âmes de ceux que j'ai chantés, fortifiez-moi, soutenez-moi, éloignez de moi le mensonge et les vapeurs corruptrices du monde, et vous, Seigneur mon Dieu! accordez-moi la grâce de produire quelques beaux vers qui me prouvent à moi-même que je ne suis pas le dernier des hommes, que je ne suis pas inférieur à ceux que je méprise!

The similarities with, and the differences from, the Pharisee's prayer are immediately obvious. The Pharisee's is one of profound self-satisfaction, whereas the poet's comes from the depths of despair and self-hatred. Henri Lemaître, wrongly according to Zimmerman, judges the prayer to be authentic by placing it in the context of Baudelaire's views on the redemptive power of art which are evident in 'Bénédiction' and have influenced so much of modern poetry right down to Eliot. But Zimmerman and Lemaître are not very far apart, and their disagreement can be overcome and resolved if the analysis of the poem is carried one step further. The prayer starts as an apparently genuine cry 'de profundis' after one of the poet's habitual 'examens de conscience', and is reminiscent of the one already quoted from 'Hygiène' in which he resolves to pray every morning to God, with his old family maid and Poe as intercessors, to give him strength to fulfil his duty. But what gives the prayer its force, and also makes it typical of the prose poems, is the sudden 'soubresaut' at the end in which he wishes to be superior to those he despises. The noble plea to God and intercessors to lift him out of his distress through the grace of artistic creation contrasts brutally with the narrow outlook which disrupts and subverts the prayer at the end and calls in doubt not only the authenticity of the spiritual exercise itself, but also, most palpably, the ideal which in *Les Fleurs du Mal* survived all the other disasters, the redemptive power of art. The final irony makes our reading of the piece, to say the least, problematic, since it calls in question the 'examen de conscience' which the poem is meant to celebrate, and yet by a curious detour the prose poem itself might be taken as an example of the kind of artistic creation which precisely proves the poet's superiority, though plainly it is not in the 'beaux vers' the prayer asks for. Indeed, the piece is written in the most wilfully prosaic style, and the poet's apparent inability to create even a few lines of fine verse indicates that he is damned to remain with the banal vulgarities he despises, without the consolation of a glimpse into a higher reality which might be accorded by a lyrical outburst, however brief. The 'morale désagréable' which emerges casts doubt upon that superiority which, even if attained, would be seen as morally indefensible, and we are left with the uncomfortable picture of the poet trapped within a hell of imperfection in which the light of 'la conscience dans le Mal' shines much more dimly than in 'L'Irrémédiable', since it illumines less a means of salvation than the satanic pride and arrogance which damned Lucifer himself. If Satan could pray, his prayer might not differ much from this one which is uttered in the depths of the night.

The sense of moral uncertainty is strong in 'Mademoiselle Bistouri' which also ends with a prayer which is ambiguous. The story, whose macabre content fixes on the fantasies of a deranged mind presenting an obvious parallel with Poe, concerns the poet's encounter during his promenade in Paris with a bizarre lady of pleasure, who presents a vast sophistication of the Romantic commonplace of the good-hearted whore. She insists in spite of his irritated protests that he must be a doctor until, succumbing to his sense of mystery and his love of the bizarre, he accompanies her to her lodging where she regales him with mulled wine and cigars in front of a brightly burning fire. It is then that gradually he learns of her curious obsession with sex and surgery, which gives her her nickname and which leads her to fantasize that her favourite *interne* should visit her 'avec sa trousse et son tablier, même avec un peu de sang dessus'.[69] Like the poet, the reader is unable to explain the mystery of motive and to reconcile the coexistence in the same person of so much gentleness and such a violent and sick imagination. Her tenderness is evident in her actions and in her speech, and her innocence emerges from her astonishment that one of the doctors had been so cruel as to denounce to the government those wounded insurrectionists whom he had treated at the hospital: 'Comment est-ce possible qu'un si bel homme ait si peu de cœur?' The question is reminiscent of the angel of pity's tremulous half-question half-statement to Satan in Vigny's 'Eloa': 'Puisque vous êtes beau, vous êtes bon, sans doute', as if beauty, truth, and goodness were indissoluble. But Mademoiselle Bistouri's question has wider implications, bristling with paradoxes which concern both the doctor and herself. How indeed can a man whose life is dedicated to healing hand over the patient he has cared for to his executioners? Is it mere heartlessness, made possible by a complete disjoining of professional and humanitarian conscience from the sense of social duty which, in turn, is based upon a certain, reactionary, notion of what society should be like? How can two such conflicting values coexist in the same man? Baudelaire does not explore these problems, which he is content to raise here in the context of the medical profession, and he leaves the reader to speculate on possible explanations. But what is even more interesting is that the question bends back on Mademoiselle Bistouri herself. How can such a gentle person be so preoccupied with surgery and its attendant physical violence? Her admiration for one of the doctors—'En voilà un homme qui aime couper, tailler et rogner!'— is expressed in terms one might expect from an enthusiastic and dedicated sadist. How are we to understand the links between madness and kindness, between prostitution and innocence, between sex and surgery? The implication is of course that in eroticism one partner appears to 'operate' upon the other, the resulting 'sadism' of which has been analysed in their various very differing ways by Sade, Laclos, Malraux, and Sartre, to name but a few. We have already drawn attention to the famous scene at Monjouvain in which Proust shows how the very sensitive can enter the inhuman world of pleasure only by putting themselves imaginatively into the skin of evil people; so that the tension between the inhuman violence of sex and the sensitivity of the 'âme tendre' is temporarily overcome by the suppression of the sensibility. The solution of this conflict in 'Mademoiselle Bistouri' is more radical and permanent, since it is provided by her insanity, the loss of reason enabling her gentleness and her erotic and sado-masochistic fantasies to coexist. 'Peux-tu te souvenir de l'époque et de l'occasion où est née en toi cette passion si particulière?' asks the poet whose tone has switched from detached curiosity and surly impatience to pity; but she has no recollection, and we are left to speculate on the possible trauma which could have produced such an innocent monster.

Like the prayer in 'A une heure du matin', the one which ends 'Mademoiselle Bistouri' is ambiguous, being both a cry of distress and a veiled indictment of the justice of an omniscient God:

La vie fourmille de monstres innocents. — Seigneur, mon Dieu! vous, le Créateur, vous, le Maître; vous qui avez fait la Loi et la Liberté; vous, le souverain qui laissez faire, vous, le juge qui pardonnez; vous qui êtes plein de motifs et de causes, et qui avez peut-être mis dans mon esprit le goût de l'horreur pour convertir mon cœur, comme la guérison au bout d'une lame; Seigneur, ayez pitié, ayez pitié des fous et des folles! O Créateur! peut-il exister des monstres aux yeux de Celui-là seul qui sait pourquoi ils existent, comment ils *se sont faits* et comment ils auraient pu *ne pas se faire*?

The prayer is curiously problematic not just for the hidden challenge to God's goodness implicit in the affirmation of her innocence, but because of the mixture of register in the vocabulary and style. The serious apostrophe to God the Creator appears somewhat diminished by the use of the expression 'le Maître' which has colloquial over-tones, and even more by the addition of the phrases about the God who has made Law and Liberty and who is full of motives and causes. These phrases seem to be in contradiction with each other, since Liberty, with its ironical capital L, seems hardly compatible with the motives and causes which, perhaps unknown to us, direct our actions according to God's inscrutable plan ('qui avez peut-être mis dans mon esprit le goût de l'horreur pour convertir mon cœur'). What freedom can the 'monstre innocent' who is Mademoiselle Bistouri enjoy in her madness? What Law has she transgressed to merit such a punishment? The poet seems to be stating categorically that God knows why such monsters exist, how they have made themselves like that, and how they could have chosen not to have made themselves like that, drawing attention to their freedom of choice by italicizing the verbs, as if men were responsible for their lives and destinies. But the story has posited the innocence of the girl, who, in any case, has no recollection of how and why her strange obsession began, so that if she is being punished it is without knowledge of her sin or of the Law that is punishing her. Madness, which Baudelaire greatly feared towards the end of his life as his malady progressed ('Maintenant j'ai toujours le vertige, et aujourd'hui

23 janvier 1862, j'ai subi un singulier avertissement, j'ai senti passer sur moi *le vent de l'aile de l'imbécillité*),[70] is the ultimate scandal, since it places the chaos of the world within man himself and at the same time, worse than stupidity, which after all may be temporary or sporadic, extinguishes the only light which lends human beings any dignity. The prayer which seems to plead in favour of innocent monsters is as much a challenge to the existence of divine providence and order, as an indication of submission and belief in their reality; it borders on the blasphemous, and like, for example, the much less sombre 'Les Dons des fées', where various gifts are given to the most unsuitable people (the gift of money and riches to one who is already rich and has no sense of charity, the love of the beautiful and poetry to a 'sombre gueux' with no means of exploiting it, the priceless gift of pleasing to those incapable of understanding its value), it points not to providence but to a moral anarchy at the heart of the universe.

III

The Poetry of Prose

Like Hugo and Gautier before him,[1] Baudelaire on occasion introduces a line of prose into his verse, for example, in 'Les Aveugles' 'Je dis: Que cherchent-ils au Ciel, tous ces aveugles?', or the opening lines of 'Le Flacon':

> Il est de forts parfums pour qui toute matière
> Est poreuse. On dirait qu'ils pénètrent le verre.

There are several reasons for such intrusions: the poet may wish simply to vary the tone, to strike a note of naïvety or 'sincerity', to provide a contrast to set off a more poetic line, or he may feel that the subject-matter, the depiction in the poems of the 'Tableaux parisiens' section of Les Fleurs du Mal of the disharmony of life in a modern capital city, for example, calls for a correspondingly unharmonious and dislocated prosody.[2] In La Fanfarlo, written in the mid-1840s, there is a curious episode which shows that the relationship between prose and poetry and the possibilities of some kind of overlap between the two genres are a preoccupation which dates from very early in his literary career. In this short story a young dandy, wishing to impress a married lady and to win her affections, presents her with a copy of his volume of sonnets with the chilling title Les Orfraies. But the stratagem misfires, and the lady is unmoved by a collection so clearly marked by the unhealthy and macabre features of second-generation Romanticism with its funereal subject-matter, anatomical descriptions, and satanic 'hommes fatals'. She enjoins him to admire the flowers in the park, whose beauty and freshness she clearly prefers to his sinister flowers of evil; whereupon the young man tries another tack, and begins to 'mettre en prose et à déclamer quelques mauvaises stances composées dans sa première manière'. This time the lady is moved, and his stratagem appears to be successful, though one can never be sure, since the interlocking of irony and literary *poncif* is extremely intricate and subtle. At first sight, at least, the reason for his success appears simple; the subject of his early poems dealing with memory, youth, innocence, a childhood paradise, and the inevitable waning of love through the realities of time and experience, is acceptable because it conforms to the aesthetic preferences of this lover of pretty flowers and the novels of Walter Scott.

But why the passage from poetry to prose? Why not quote the 'mauvaises stances' directly, since they conform to her literary tastes? An obvious explanation would be that they are so bad technically that a prose rendering would be a certain improvement; in which case Valéry's declaration that to put a poem into prose 'c'est tout simplement méconnaître l'essence d'un art',[3] would be inoperative, simply because the verse had not attained the status of art. Critics have drawn attention to the presence in this passage of four lines from Baudelaire's own early poetry:

Il aimait à la voir, avec ses jupes blanches,
Courir tout au travers du feuillage et des branches,
Gauche et pleine de grâce, alors qu'elle cachait
Sa jambe, si sa robe aux buissons s'accrochait...[4]

They are 'translated' as follows: 'c'est l'heure où les jardins sont pleins de robes roses et blanches qui ne craignent pas de se mouiller. Les buissons complaisants accrochent les jupes fuyantes, les cheveux bruns et les boucles blondes se mêlent en tourbillonnant.' The prose here is a distinct improvement on the third-rate poetry, and there is no attempt to deflate the Romantic rhetoric by a prosaic rhythm, as has been argued convincingly for a later passage in the story,[5] which is spoken by the ironic narrator. After all the passionate Samuel Cramer, 'à qui la phrase et la période étaient venues', is intent on impressing Mme de Cosmelly by his sincerity. However, what is noteworthy about Samuel's long speech are the many echoes we find in it not just of Baudelaire's earlier works, such as the above fragment and 'J'aime le souvenir de ces époques nues',[6] but from ones which were almost certainly all written later, in particular 'Harmonie du soir' and 'Mœsta et errabunda'; so that a perfectly good authorial reason for the use of prose is that the verse poems did not yet exist, no doubt because at this stage Baudelaire had not evolved a style and a vision to lift the subject-matter above the level of a literary commonplace. But for all that, the decision to put the poems into prose has to be motivated and explained within the context of the story and of Samuel's strategy of seduction. He could just as easily, one supposes, have extemporized his diatribe, since he is already 'worked up' linguistically and since, in any case, Mme de Cosmelly is not aware of the existence of the poems written in his first manner. No reason is given for the recourse to prose, and we are forced to speculate, bearing in mind the demands of the context.

Though Mme de Cosmelly is shown to favour the pure and healthy form of early Romanticism, in her criticism she shows common sense and a certain ironic realism in revealing the silliness of poets like Samuel in ecstasies before 'les sultanes de bas lieu, qui doivent, ce me semble, à l'aspect de la délicate personne d'un poète, ouvrir des yeux aussi grands que des bestiaux qui se réveillent dans un incendie'. How does one set about seducing through literature such a hard-headed woman with a taste for incongruous comparisons, who, at the same time, is given to Romantic nostalgia and yearning? Now, the text makes it clear that Samuel succeeds not just because he has struck the right aesthetic note, but because, in a way he could not have predicted, he has struck a nerve, in particular with his reference to the transitory nature of love; so that her tears, which he naïvely and arrogantly regards as his literary property, are shown to be the result of a felicitous encounter between literature and experience. Samuel's somewhat high-flown speech moves her because she interprets his words about memory, childhood, and loss of innocence, in the light of her present unhappiness caused by her husband's infidelity and the contrast it provides with past happiness. Her emotion appears real, not aesthetic. But one might also argue that she is moved because Samuel's poetic prose, by appearing spontaneous and 'sincere' (whereas a passage in verse would stand out as if in quotation marks as art and, consequently, as being bracketed off from reality), has allowed her to identify herself more closely with the descriptions, memories, and sentiments it evokes. For all its romantic exclamations, ternary sentences, and 'enflure', it is able to appear more intimately and more directly linked to real experience and to life, in short, to have a greater degree of referentiality than verse would have, and certainly than the later poems which came out of it. 'Harmonie du soir' and 'Mœsta et errabunda', which are among the most lyrical of the poet's production, belong to the domain

of beauty rather than experience, to the domain of eternity, as
Jacques Rivière would have it, rather than to time: 'Dans un beau
poème il n'y a jamais progression: la fin est toujours au même
niveau que le commencement [. . .]. L'émotion poétique est une
sorte de tournoiement par lequel se reforme en nous, au milieu de
la fuite même des choses, une flaque d'éternité.'[7] The paradoxes of
the passage seem endless, for the reader is meant to see through
Samuel's abuse of literary cliché, but is at the same time aware
that the clichés have been given value and authenticity by being
put into a speech which is supposedly improvised during a real
conversation—taking place, of course, within a highly self-conscious
work of literature.[8] We can never leave the 'literariness' of the
text; but we can sense that a possible strategy behind the use of
prose is to persuade by its apparently greater immediacy and truth,
and it is tempting to conclude that, even at this very early stage,
when no prose experiments had yet been produced, Baudelaire
had in mind, however vaguely, the same motives and the same
strategy as Samuel Cramer: to make the matter of poetry more
persuasive and more present by immersing it in the contingent world
of experience.

   In *Du vin et du hachisch* of 1851 we are on surer ground, and
can replace speculation by observation. Here Baudelaire adopts
the curious procedure of translating 'L'Âme du vin' more or less
directly into prose, and transposing 'Le Vin des chiffonniers'[9] and
incorporating it into his narrative. The conscious reasons for this
procedure and the author's intentions are unknown, there being no
statement of them either in the essay itself or in the correspondence.
It may well be that the principal reason, as Claude Pichois has pointed
out, was the poet's creative difficulty, lack of inspiration, and
shortage of copy, self-imitation being a constant feature of his
work.[10] Whatever the reason, the experiment can be seen as further
evidence of his preoccupation with the frontiers of prose and poetry,
with their different functions, and with the changes which are required
in a translation or transposition. Although the translation follows
the original poem very closely and keeps to a large extent a stanzaic
structure (the last three stanzas are set out as separate paragraphs),
and although there is no attempt to play down the fiction of the wine
addressing itself to man, what is distinctive about the prose version
is the increase in detail and elaboration. For example, the fifth stanza
which reads

> J'allumerai les yeux de ta femme ravie;
> A ton fils je rendrai sa force et ses couleurs
> Et serai pour ce frêle athlète de la vie
> L'huile qui raffermit les muscles des lutteurs.

is almost doubled in length:

> J'allumerai les yeux de ta vieille femme, la vieille compagne de tes chagrins journaliers et de tes plus vieilles espérances. J'attendrirai son regard et je mettrai au fond de sa prunelle l'éclair de sa jeunesse. Et ton cher petit, tout pâlot, ce pauvre petit ânon attelé à la même fatigue que le limonier, je lui rendrai les belles couleurs de son berceau, et je serai pour ce nouvel athlète de la vie l'huile qui raffermissait les muscles des anciens lutteurs.

The picture both of the mother and of the son is much more detailed[11] in the 'freer' prose translation which is unencumbered by rhyme and rhythm. Furthermore, there is already a deliberate attempt to prevent any rhythmical element from the poetry being carried over into the prose, as the translation of the third and fourth lines of the stanza indicates. The prose follows the verse almost word for word, but the very minor alterations, the replacement of 'frêle' by 'nouvel', 'raffermit' by 'raffermissait', and the addition of 'anciens' to 'lutteurs', have the effect of disrupting the alexandrine and producing a prose rhythm. This technique seems almost gratuitously wilful as when the last line of the previous stanza, 'Tu me glorifieras et tu seras content', which could perfectly well have remained as it stood, is rendered 'tu me glorifieras fièrement, et tu seras vraiment content', where the adverbs, particularly the second one, which are technically intensifiers, have, as in conversational speech, the opposite effect of weakening or banalizing the statement. These alterations would appear to stem not from a desire to conform to Vaugelas's and Marmontel's proscription of verse in prose, but from a deliberate attempt to create a muted and featureless style.[12]

The prose and verse treatment of the theme of twilight in the two 'Crépuscule du soir' poems, published in the *Hommage à C. F. Denecourt* of 1855, have undergone a very close analysis.[13] Detecting in the verse poem certain prosaic elements such as enjambment and formal dislocation to evoke the disharmony of Parisian life, and in the prose poem poetic elements such as a form of stanzaic structure, ternary sentences, and antithetical balance, the writer concludes that the juxtaposition of the two poems raises the question of the interpenetrability of prose and poetry rather than reinforcing the belief that they must be kept separate. I would not wish to disagree with this conclusion, except to emphasize that the 'ton raisonneur' which, it is rightly claimed, Baudelaire cultivates in the prose poem is strengthened, rather than poeticized, by the somewhat restricted ternary rhythms which have none of the expansiveness characteristic of, for example, the early Flaubert. Indeed, the sentences tend to be short, even staccato; there is little syntactic variety, and there could be few statements more devoid of poetry than 'La venue du soir gâtait les meilleures choses', or the concluding sentence which seems to tail off rather than to produce a punch line: 'Et, bien qu'il ne soit pas rare de voir la même cause engendrer deux effets contraires, cela m'intrigue et m'étonne toujours.' In addition, it is important to contrast the images and sensations of the verse poem—evening arriving like a criminal, demons hovering in the night air, flickering gaslight with 'la Prostitution [qui] s'allume dans la rue', night grasping us by the throat—with the thoughts and sentiments which are evoked in the prose.[14] For example, in the opening stanza the appeal to the eye is minimal:

> La tombée de la nuit a toujours été pour moi le signal d'une fête intérieure et comme la délivrance d'une angoisse. Dans les bois comme dans les rues d'une grande ville, l'assombrissement du jour et le pointillement des étoiles ou des lanternes éclairent mon esprit.

—and the rest of the poem has a distinctly anecdotal quality whose appeal is to the intellect rather than to the imagination of the reader. There is no attempt at the famous 'sorcellerie évocatoire' or the 'magie suggestive',[15] whereby an object in the external world becomes the vehicle for the emotion of the poem and at the same time, as in the painting of Delacroix, appeals to the imagination and to the affective memory of the reader. It is clear, even at this very early stage, that in the prose working of the theme of twilight Baudelaire is moving towards the creation of a poetry not of images and sensations, which is the 'tour de force' of *Les Fleurs du Mal*, but towards a prose poetry of ideas.

The doublets of 1857—'La Chevelure' and 'Un hémisphère dans une chevelure', and the two 'Invitation au voyage'—have received much critical comment, notably from Gertrud Streit, Crépet and Blin, Ratermanis, and most recently by Barbara Johnson in the most persuasive section of her *Défigurations du langage poétique*, and it would be idle to restate what has been already so well established.[16]

In particular, Barbara Johnson's contribution has been to show the way in which metaphor gives way to metonymy in the prose pieces, how the poetic language and values in 'L'Invitation au voyage' are debased by being 'mercantalized', and how the prose versions can be read as a kind of 'send-up' of their verse counterparts and the poetic values they celebrate. What should be stressed is the way in which the prose doublets of 1857 exemplify, in their different manners and with differing degrees of emphasis, elements which have already emerged from our discussion of *Du vin et du hachisch* and the two 'Crépuscules', that is to say, the increase in detail (the prose 'Invitation' is ninety-three lines long in Kopp's edition compared with the forty-two brief lines of the verse with their refrain), the playing down of imagery and sensation, and the increased variety of rhythm and tone.

Suzanne Bernard has lamented[17] over the impoverishment of the penultimate stanza of 'La Chevelure':

> Cheveux bleus, pavillon de ténèbres tendues,
> Vous me rendez l'azur du ciel immense et rond.

These splendid lines contain a boundless reverie in which the long tresses of the woman's black hair, described in an earlier stanza as an ebony sea, take on the colour of the sea itself, and at the same time are dreamt of as providing protection, sensuality, and mystery. In the second line the sensuous gives way to the mystical as the imagery opens out in an evocation of the immensity of the azure blue sky with its associations of infinity, purity, and elevation, but it is an infinity with nothing awesome or overpowering about it, an infinity which is round, denoting protection, completion, and oneness. Like Wordsworth's 'round air',[18] the image is not just a phenomenon of perception whereby the heavens appear to the eye as a rounded vault; the roundness has a moral quality adding a sense of completion and unity to that of protection and confinement. But in the prose version the blue hair with its 'pavillon' of darkness, the sensuality and mystery, and the round sky, are replaced by two very plain statements which are essentially abstract and featureless:

> Dans l'ardent foyer de ta chevelure, je respire l'odeur du tabac mêlé à l'opium et au sucre; dans la nuit de ta chevelure, je vois resplendir l'infini de l'azur tropical.

The first statement adds further exotic smells to the 'huile de coco', 'musc', and 'goudron' which are present in both verse and prose (though the latter is careful not to reproduce the rhythms of the alexandrine), while in the second statement the appeal has moved away from the senses, as in 'Le Crépuscule du soir', in the direction of the intellect, from image to idea. What imagery there is in the prose pieces is either played down and made anodyne as here, or is literalized in a manner which is calculated to shock, as in the extraordinary 'je mange des souvenirs' which replaces 'la gourde / Où je hume à longs traits le vin du souvenir', with the result that, as Barbara Johnson has noted,[19] the poetic is banalized rather than the prosaic being poeticized.

Something very similar is happening in the prose 'Invitation au voyage' which develops the 'meubles luisants, / Polis par les ans' of the verse into the most extraordinary description of this land of Cocagne, 'où tout est riche, propre et luisant, comme une belle conscience, comme une magnifique batterie de cuisine, comme une splendide orfèvrerie, comme une bijouterie bariolée!' Such similes by far outdo those Yankee 'comparaisons énormes'[20] like 'la nuit s'épaississait ainsi qu'une cloison', the 'serpent qui danse au bout d'un bâton', the woman's bosom which is compared to a 'belle armoire' which Laforgue admired, in both senses of the word, in *Les Fleurs du Mal*, and which he thought were as astonishing and as daring as those which are to be found in the Song of Songs. Here the gap between tenor and vehicle is so wide as to be grotesque or absurd, it has something of the violence and the humour of the notorious 'beau comme' of Lautréamont which were to delight the Surrealists, for example, 'comme la rencontre fortuite sur une table de dissection d'une machine à coudre et d'un parapluie'.[21] The effect of the figure is to undermine figurality and the whole notion of poetry upon which it rests, and far from being projected into a reverie in which oppositions are reduced through correspondence and analogy as when reading the verse poems, the reader is confronted with a grotesque world of incompatibilities. The technique here is not so much that of the poetic image, but rather of jokes or of humour, since as Jean-Paul Richter put it, 'joking is the disguised priest who weds every couple', or as Kraepelin has it, it is 'the arbitrary connecting or linking [. . .] of two ideas which in some way contrast with each other.'[22] Of course, a conscience can be clear and pure, and so can kitchen pots and pans; but the two belong to such different linguistic and cultural codes that their juxtaposition and fundamental incompatibility are at once grotesque and funny. The effect of such intrusions, together with the familiar tone—'Un vrai pays de Cocagne, te dis-je'—is to provide one of these 'soubresauts de la conscience' which in his 'dédicace' to Arsène Houssaye Baudelaire thought it was the function of the prose poem to convey. The intention and the effect are clearly ironic and deflating.

As another example we may take the third last stanza of 'Un hémisphère dans une chevelure', where the irony is evident in the cacophony of 'les langueurs des longues heures', and especially in the degrading of the dream of a sexual and mystical rapture in the 'Infinis bercements du loisir embaumé' to the banal and lazy pleasure of being swayed in a cabin 'entre les pots de fleurs et les gargoulettes rafraîchissantes'. Until recently, the effect of such shifts of tone in the 1857 doublets has not been sufficiently stressed: the juxtaposition of the ironic or sarcastic and the lyrical, which in any case is rarely unalloyed, and often undermined by a deflating epithet such as 'honnête' applied to the exotic dream of a European China, is essentially negative, since the realistic destroys the ideal, the prosaic destroys the lyrical. Once again, it is clear that, in such circumstances and with such a mixture of tones, the opposite, that is to say the recuperation of the prosaic by the lyrical, just does not take place. The irony in these doublets stems from our realization of the folly of trying to give presence to what is by definition absent and unattainable, as if the ideal could actually be made to exist. The notion is a grotesque contradiction, and inevitably, once inserted into the real world of time and matter, the ideal is reduced to a banal commodity, sought after with all the frenzy of the vulgar and rapacious. As Baudelaire himself put it in another quite different context, though the idea remains the same, what would we do with our eternal souls if the dream were made into reality?[23]

A similar ironic intention is also clear in another of the prose poems published in 1857, called 'Les Projets', where the poet tries to imagine his mistress in various costumes and situations, abandoning each one in turn and finally accepting the superiority of dreams over reality. But what is amusing is that each dream is a well-worn literary commonplace which we are meant to see through and thereby feel a sense of superiority over the narrator who remains a victim of his own naïve illusions. The décor of his projects is variously aristocratic with palaces and gardens, tropical with Portuguese rococo furniture, exotic birds, chattering negresses, and strange, gleaming trees, and finally rustic with a modest but clean inn offering rough sheets and wine, simple food, and brightly coloured crockery. Furthermore, the exclamation 'c'est *là* qu'il faudrait demeurer pour cultiver le rêve de ma vie' is doubly ironic since it refers us back to the repeated 'c'est là' of 'L'Invitation au voyage'. All these projects correspond to different features of Romantic escapism, and the poet's irony is delicately underscored by the dead-pan narration, and the sudden and gratuitous changes from one fantasy to another, each one introduced by a paragraph beginning with 'Et' in order to convey the sense of an unending and facile stream of clichés. The poem ends ostensibly on a choice for virtuality over reality and action, as the poet returns home 'à cette heure où les conseils de la Sagesse ne sont plus étouffés par les bourdonnements de la vie extérieure', complacently asking himself, 'Pourquoi contraindre mon corps à changer de place, puisque mon âme voyage si lestement? Et à quoi bon exécuter des projets, puisque le projet est en lui-même une jouissance suffisante?' But it would be wrong to think that at this point the poet had exhausted his irony, which, on the contrary, continues to the end of the poem, mocking the banal wisdom of remaining within the four walls of a room, as in 'La Solitude', and the preference for dream over reality, with the result that at the end nothing is celebrated, and no values are made to emerge apart from that of stating the problematical nature of values. Once again, Baudelaire's undermining of a cliché has left us with a 'morale désagréable', and a view of all human aspirations and actions as vanity and 'divertissement', and I would suggest that Suzanne Bernard was possibly missing the point in preferring the lyrical outburst of the original conclusion of the poem and in seeing in what she took to be 'transformations dans le sens de la platitude,'[24] a waning of Baudelaire's creative imagination. On the contrary, what we are witnessing is a deepening of his pessimism and a development of his aesthetic of the prose poem.

Several essential and closely related elements would then appear to emerge from Baudelaire's experiments in *La Fanfarlo* and *Du vin et du hachisch*, and from the prose poems of 1857: prose is more suited to the expression of truth than to the creation of beauty, in the prose poem the writer will be more detailed and discursive, he will avoid the rhythms of verse, and will cultivate a neutral style, he will play down metaphor and imagery, and appeal more to the

intellect than to the imagination and the senses, and he will vary
the tone through the intrusion of 'soubresauts' and the ironic clash
of linguistic and cultural register. In studying Baudelaire's production
of prose poetry we are aware of uncertainties and hesitations, and
the wide spectrum of style and sub-genre ranging from the idiosyn-
cratic lyricism of the doublets to anecdotes, allegories, 'boutades',
essays, and lengthy and digressive stories such as 'Le Mauvais Vitrier'
and 'Mademoiselle Bistouri', fosters the suspicion that its evolution
owes more to accident than to design. But whatever the chronological
evolution of his practice, an analysis of the early works up to 1857
indicates that the fundamental principles of the theory were present
from a very early stage, and that with differing degrees of emphasis,
and in varying combinations, they preside over his practice until the
very last poems. There is in the *Notes nouvelles sur Edgar Poe* of
1857 a passage on the aesthetic of the short story, the principal points
of which bear such a remarkable similarity to the ones we have just
made concerning the prose poem that it would be proper to quote
it 'in extenso':

Il est un point par lequel la nouvelle a une supériorité, même sur le poème.
Le rythme est nécessaire au développement de l'idée de beauté, qui est le
but le plus grand et le plus noble du poème. Or, les artifices du rythme sont
un obstacle insurmontable à ce développement minutieux de pensées et
d'expressions qui a pour objet la *vérité*. Car la vérité peut être souvent le
but de la nouvelle, et le raisonnement, le meilleur outil pour la construction
d'une nouvelle parfaite. C'est pourquoi ce genre de composition qui n'est
pas situé à une aussi grande élévation que la poésie pure, peut fournir des
produits plus variés et plus facilement appréciables pour le commun des
lecteurs. De plus, l'auteur d'une nouvelle a à sa disposition une multitude de
tons, de nuances de langage, le ton raisonneur, le sarcastique, l'humoristique,
que répudie la poésie, et qui sont comme des dissonances, des outrages à
l'idée de beauté pure. Et c'est aussi ce qui fait que l'auteur qui poursuit dans
une nouvelle un simple but de beauté ne travaille qu'à son grand désavantage,
privé qu'il est de l'instrument le plus utile, le rythme. Je sais que dans toutes
les littératures des efforts ont été faits, souvent heureux, pour créer des contes
purement poétiques; Edgar Poe lui-même en a fait de très beaux. Mais ce
sont des luttes et des efforts qui ne servent qu'à démontrer la force des vrais
moyens adaptés aux buts correspondants, et je serais pas éloigné de croire
que chez quelques auteurs, les plus grands qu'on puisse choisir, ces tentations
héroïques vinssent d'un désespoir.[25]

Although, like the often quoted sentence from the 1859 *Salon* about
the dangers of fantasy, 'dangereuse comme la poésie en prose',[26] the

end of this passage shows Baudelaire sceptical about any mingling of the genres, it is tempting, given the similarities mentioned above, to substitute in the passage 'prose poem' for 'short story', and to think that he had clearly worked out the direction he wished to take and that he had already established the prose poem on a solid foundation of consciously held principles.

But given the hesitations we have already mentioned and the fact that he published no more prose poems for four years until 1861, the reality was most likely to have been much less defined and clear cut, and it would take many more years of experimentation before the elements we have noted in his practice were formed into a coherent aesthetic.

However that may be, it is clear that from the beginning Baudelaire was not seeking a means in prose to convey the lofty themes of Romantic poetry or the kind of lyricism which was to find expression in *Les Fleurs du Mal*. If the first two paragraphs of section III 'De la couleur' of the *Salon* of 1846 are to be considered his first prose poem, as has been suggested,[27] then it would be a prose poem based on a totally different aesthetic from the one which governed the rest of his production. One would be on safer ground to think of it as a 'purple patch' using all the power of imagery and rhetoric to put forward his ideas about the nature of colour. There is little trace, even in his early experiments, of a desire to create a poetic prose like Chateaubriand's or of the kind exemplified in Flaubert's description of Chateaubriand's grave at Saint-Malo:

Il dormira là-dessous, la tête tournée vers la mer; dans ce sépulcre bâti sur un écueil, son immortalité sera comme fut sa vie, déserte des autres et tout entourée d'orages. Les vagues avec les siècles murmureront longtemps autour de ce grand souvenir; dans les tempêtes elles bondiront jusqu'à ses pieds, ou les matins d'été, quand les voiles blanches se déploient et que l'hirondelle arrive d'au delà des mers, longues et douces, elles lui apporteront la volupté mélancolique des horizons et la caresse des larges brises. Et les jours ainsi s'écoulant, pendant que les flots de la grève natale iront se balançant toujours entre son berceau et son tombeau, le cœur de René devenu froid, lentement, s'éparpillera dans le néant, au rythme sans fin de cette musique éternelle.[28]

There is nothing resembling this kind of solemn and univocal meditation in the prose poems. The rising and falling cadences, the expansive ternary sentences, the rolling undulation of the syntax with the intercalated phrases and subordinate clauses forming a kind of orchestration which the reader might be tempted to conduct, are nowhere echoed in the prose poems, unless in the curiously anomalous addition to the final version of 'Le Crépuscule du soir' published in 1864. Such an explosion of lyricism is rare and if we are to believe Suzanne Bernard, as the present writer does, is an infelicitous intrusion;[29] for the lyricism at the beginning of 'Le *Confiteor* de l'artiste' or 'La Chambre double' is more restrained, staccato, and mixed in phonetic and thematic tone; the rhythms are less elaborate, the word order is simpler, and the vocabulary seems colourless in comparison. In spite of his intention of creating, as he claims in the 'Dédicace' to Houssaye, a poetic prose which can adapt to the 'mouvements lyriques de l'âme, aux ondulations de la rêverie, aux soubresauts de la conscience', the emphasis falls increasingly upon disharmony rather than on moments of lyrical 'envol' (on what, in his essays on Delacroix and Banville, he called 'ces beaux jours de l'esprit'),[30] which, in any case, often appear to restrain or cut short a promised effusion. Often, as in 'Les Bienfaits de la lune', the lyricism seems to be consciously overdone, and, in any case, the juxtaposition of the lyrical and the banal or strident tends to act as an ironic comment on the former. In 'Any where out of the world' the evocation of the northern wastes at the extreme end of the Baltic is marked by the same kind of irony as we found in 'Les Projets', since it follows similar references to stock exotic sites likely to appeal to a mind bent upon distraction, which the poet dismisses as a form of physical and mental 'déménagement'. Even the lyrical effusion itself—'Là, nous pourrons prendre de longs bains de ténèbres, cependant que, pour nous divertir, les aurores boréales nous enverront de temps en temps leurs gerbes roses, comme des reflets d'un feu d'artifice de l'Enfer!'—is undermined not least by the northern lights which, instead of bearing witness to the beauty and wonders of nature, are likened to some kind of infernal firework display. The move towards prose poetry is intended to enable the poet to give expression to the 'soubresauts de la conscience' and to the disharmony of modern man subject to the spleen and stridency of life in a vast modern capital. Baudelaire's technique differs, then, totally from that of Rimbaud, for example, who, feeling that traditional prosody, which had reached its highest lyrical expression with the Parnasse, had become exhausted, sought ellipsis and greater compression of meaning, the sudden illumination from the extra-ordinary image, the disruption of grammar, syntax, and logical development, the short-circuiting of meaning, new rhythms and harmonies, since 'les inventions d'inconnu réclament des formes nouvelles'.[31] Baudelaire, on the other hand, highlights the prosaic quality of his pieces in the search for disharmony. The realism and 'truth' of his subject-matter require a different medium from verse, which, however much one may disrupt its rhythms, by enjambment and by shifting the caesura, always returns to some kind of harmony, no matter how unsure, with the regular completion of the even line—octosyllable, decasyllable, alexandrine—together with the inevitable and reassuring return of the rhyme. Baudelaire did not envisage the possibilities of the uneven nine- or eleven-syllable line (the latter in the hand of Rimbaud and Verlaine could be used to convey the most chaotic sensations and feelings as in 'Michel et Christine' and 'Crimen Amoris'),[32] nor did he envisage the use of assonance and counter-assonance to replace regular rhyme. He saw prose as the medium for the real as opposed to the ideal, and for detail and irony, and the description of the prose poems which he gives to Troubat in 1866—'encore *Les Fleurs du Mal*, mais avec beaucoup plus de liberté, et de détail, et de raillerie'[33] is tantamount to a form of anti-poetry, when set against contemporary poetic norms.

A natural consequence of this attitude towards form is that very many of the poems make fun of more established poetic and literary attitudes and can be read as a kind of intertextual debunking. Take, for example, the beginning of 'Le Gâteau' which appears at first reading to be a perfectly serious meditation:

Je voyageais. Le paysage au milieu duquel j'étais placé était d'une grandeur et d'une noblesse irrésistibles. Il en passa sans doute en ce moment quelque chose dans mon âme. Mes pensées voltigeaient avec une légèreté égale à celle de l'atmosphère; les passions vulgaires, telles que la haine et l'amour profane, m'apparaissaient maintenant aussi éloignées que les nuées qui défilaient au fond des abîmes sous mes pieds; mon âme me semblait aussi vaste et aussi pure que la coupole du ciel dont j'étais enveloppé; le souvenir des choses terrestres n'arrivait à mon cœur qu'affaibli et diminué, comme le son de la clochette des bestiaux imperceptibles qui paissaient loin, bien loin, sur le versant d'une autre montagne. Sur le petit lac immobile, noir de son immense profondeur, passait quelquefois l'ombre d'un nuage, comme le reflet du manteau d'un géant aérien volant à travers le ciel. Et je me souviens que cette sensation solennelle et rare, causée par un grand mouvement parfaitement silencieux, me remplissait d'une joie mêlée de peur. Bref, je me sentais, grâce à l'enthousiasmante beauté dont j'étais environné, en parfaite paix avec moi-même et avec l'univers; je crois même que, dans ma parfaite béatitude et dans mon total oubli de tout le mal terrestre, j'en étais venu à ne plus trouver si ridicules les journaux qui prétendent que l'homme est né bon.

Until he comes to the word 'Bref', which seems to indicate a sense of relief that one has reached the end of a tiresome list of well-worn ideas and sentiments, and the heavily ironic 'béatitude' to indicate the poet's state of mind, the hasty reader might be forgiven, initially at least, for not detecting the other more discreet ironies in the passage, to which he might have been alerted by the introductory 'Je voyageais', situating the piece and its dominant 'état d'âme' in the context of travel literature. The literary commonplaces abound: the elevated site corresponding to the elevation of the meditation, the references to 'la coupole du ciel' and the 'abîmes sous mes pieds', the distant echo of earthly sounds, 'enthousiasme' with its religious overtones.[34] Critics have noticed that the description has many similarities with a very early poem of Baudelaire's inspired by a visit to the Pyrenees:

> Tout là-haut, tout là-haut, loin de la route sûre,
> Des fermes, des vallons, par-delà les coteaux,
> Par-delà les forêts, les tapis de verdure,
> Loin des derniers gazons foulés par les troupeaux [. . .][35]

while others have shown the parallels of theme with those of Rousseau's *Rêveries*. But what has not, to my knowledge, been recorded is that the verse poem is an imitation of Lamartine's 'L'Isolement' and 'Le Vallon', and that 'Le Gâteau' is a parody of certain stanzas of two of Lamartine's best-known poems. The lofty mountain site and the distant lake with its reflections is reminiscent of the opening stanzas of 'L'Isolement', while the poet's 'vague-à-l'âme', the expiry of sensations at the threshold of consciousness, and the mistiness of the atmosphere provoking a movement towards introspection, echo to the point of parody some famous lines from 'Le Vallon':

> Mon cœur est en repos, mon âme est en silence!
> Le bruit lointain du monde expire en arrivant,
> Comme un son éloigné qu'affaiblit la distance,
> A l'oreille incertaine apporté par le vent.
>
> D'ici je vois la vie à travers un nuage,
> S'évanouir pour moi dans l'ombre du passé [. . .]

This parody of a well-worn Romantic theme is followed by the strident irruption of the two savage little boys fighting over a piece of bread they call cake. The myth of the child, of which we saw something in Fancioulle, and which has found so much prestige in literature since Romanticism, is brought down to a very base reality indeed. The child is no longer the inhabitant of 'le vert paradis des amours enfantines',[36] no longer the symbol of poetic genius—'le génie, n'est que l'*enfance retrouvée* à volonté'[37]—nor is he always intoxicated with some rapturous or beatific vision of a world bathed in glory. In reality, children are violent, rapacious, and greedy, they exemplify the barbarity latent in human nature, and far from being immune from original sin, they are in fact nearer to it, indulging in their struggle for the cake in a 'guerre parfaitement fratricide'.

Similarly, the Romantic glorification of women is constantly deflated by the use of the over-emphatic appellation 'mon cher ange'[38] throughout the prose poems. Love and any notion of a communion of minds are seen as aberrations; for women, like children, are selfish, savage, vulgar, and cruel, that is when they are not widows and part of the poet's spiritual family, or out of their minds like Mademoiselle Bistouri. Mothers are callous and devoid of maternal feeling, the voice of the dreaming poet's mistress, of his 'petite folle bien-aimée' is raucous, hysterical, roughened by cheap spirits, and prone to violent language as is her hand to violent action. Bénédicta, who was too good and pure to live (an obvious send-up of the Romantic heroine condemned to die young and innocent after the manner of Atala), is in reality a 'fameuse canaille'. Even in 'Le Désir de peindre' where his mistress is described as enchantingly dark and mysterious ('En elle le noir abonde: et tout ce qu'elle inspire est nocturne et profond'), and the brightness of her eyes as an 'explosion dans les ténèbres', he cannot resist a demeaning allusion to her narrow forehead inhabited by 'la volonté tenace et l'amour de la proie'. In 'Les Bienfaits de la lune', after the incantatory enumeration of all the prestigious associations of his mistress with sea, sky, silence, and night, the poet adds the most jarring and deflating 'soubresaut':

Et c'est pour cela, maudite chère enfant gâtée, que je suis maintenant couché à tes pieds, cherchant dans toute ta personne le reflet de la redoutable Divinité, de la fatidique marraine, de la nourrice empoisonneuse de tous les *lunatiques*.

The same kind of irony is exemplified in 'L'Horloge', where the poet admits to having got carried away in his description of his mistress, calling his lyrical outburst a 'madrigal vraiment méritoire, et aussi emphatique que vous-même', and thereby indicating that it was a mere literary game far removed from reality and little more than an insincere and pretentious gallantry. 'La Femme sauvage et la petite-maîtresse' and 'Portraits de maîtresses' present relationships between the sexes in a profoundly gloomy light. Even physical love is not seen as some frantic and vain search for the absolute in sensation, a misdirection of our spirituality into the flesh, but as something resembling a surgical operation, and we have seen that in 'Les Tentations' Eros is portrayed with phials of sinister liquids, gleaming knives, and surgical instruments on his belt, and Mademoiselle Bistouri is out of her mind professing a bizarre taste for doctors and surgeons with blood-stained aprons.

  The shortest poem in the collection 'Le Miroir' has attracted little critical attention, and since Lemaître's edition of 1962 it has tended to be dismissed as a 'poème-boutade', a kind of literary genre, it would seem from certain passages in the *Journaux intimes*, which Baudelaire liked to practise, and in which 'tout un monde de désillusions et de rancœurs se ramasse dans une incisive brièveté'.[39] The poem concerns a dreadfully ugly man who is given to looking at himself in the mirror. When the poet asks him why he does so, since the experience must be unpleasant, the man replies that, according to the immortal principles of 1789, all men are equal in rights, and that, consequently, he has the right to look at himself; with pleasure or displeasure is a matter for his own conscience. At this the poet concludes that 'Au nom du bon sens, j'avais sans doute raison; mais, au point de vue de la loi, il n'avait pas tort.' Lemaître suggests that the poem reflects Baudelaire's scorn of the principles of the Revolution and the dandy's hatred of masculine ugliness; in which case, his unwillingness to comment further would be justified, since there would be little point in expatiating upon an absurd and bitter piece which appears to be nothing more than a mercifully brief dialogue between imbeciles. However, such an attitude, negative and dismissive, gives no credit to Baudelaire's taste or to his literary genius. Although short of copy, he would be unlikely to publish something he thought unworthy, and though it is true that the quality of the prose poems, which gave him infinite trouble, is uneven, if we go no further than Lemaître's interpretation, then 'Le Miroir' must have a place all to itself at the nadir of the collection.

By placing the poem in the context of the literary treatment of the theme of the mirror, Kopp and Jasinski[40] have gone some way towards widening its meaning and scope. It does seem unnecessarily restrictive to interpret the mirror literally. If, on the other hand, we interpret it as a moral rather than as a real mirror, and if we place the poem in the dual context of man's desire to know himself and the dandy's cult of the beautiful in his own person, the poem gains considerably in meaning and resonance. I would suggest that Vigny's picture in 'La Maison du berger' of fallen mankind, bent upon self-love as a punishment for eating the forbidden fruit, 'Tourmenté de s'aimer, tourmenté de se voir',[41] provides a concealed, but vital, intertext which sets off the irony of the poem. So also does Baudelaire's preoccupation with mirrors; for the dandy 'doit vivre et dormir devant un miroir',[42] not in order to be flattered by the reflection of his own good looks, but in order to gain greater self-awareness, to fashion himself morally and aesthetically according to an ideal of lucidity and control, and to make of himself a protest against the laxities of natural self-indulgence. This kind of moral and aesthetic humanism is grounded in an awareness of man's fallen condition: it is like spirituality which, as Baudelaire says in the *Journaux intimes*, is a 'désir de monter en grade'.[43] If these themes and preoccupations are indeed the hidden intertext of this bizarre little poem, then the 'homme épouvantable' will be seen to consider his presence in the world to be justified by right, and since the immortal principles of '89 take no account of the notion of original sin, he would appear to be able to accept himself, whatever his (moral) ugliness, as an example of natural man. The moral rigour of the Christian and the discipline of the dandy and aesthete have been replaced by the untroubled self-acceptance of the democrat exercising his rights. The implication of the poet's assertion, that from the point of view of common sense he was right in criticizing the man, would then appear to be that the man's self-examination in the mirror is pointless, since it cannot lead to an 'examen de conscience' which is its proper function. His attitude is absurd, and there is a kind of tautology at work, since his 'examen de conscience' with pleasure or distaste only concerns his conscience. In other words, he has a right to regard his ugliness by whatever standard that moral ugliness itself may desire, and not in the light of the truly immortal principle of original sin which defines man's place both in time and society. There can be no point in such a self-examination since it will lead to no change in the individual: it is as if the Devil had turned into Narcissus in a world where mirrors do not have the kindness to shatter. There is an element of gross farce about the poem which, far from showing Baudelaire's anger, as has been alleged, with the principles of '89 and the apotheosis of individual and democratic values, shows him reducing them to absurdity and dismissing them with a quip and a pirouette.

It will appear in no way surprising that, given Baudelaire's increasing preoccupation with ideas and with the ironic subversion of established poetic attitudes and themes, he should move increasingly towards the creation of prose poems which are predominantly prosaic in vocabulary, syntax, imagery, and theme. Many attempts have been made to classify the prose poems in addition to the poet's, which can be found in the 'Reliquat'.[44] The most recent classification,[45] among the most convincing, puts only seventeen pieces under the heading 'poem', which includes all of the six poems published in 1855 and 1857. The rest, which are distributed with commendable tentativeness under the headings 'Poétique', 'Poème-boutade', 'Moralité', 'Essai', and 'Conte', can all be seen to be essentially narrative or expository in their differing ways. Now, as this movement towards narration and exposition, which both Baudelaire and Sartre[46] see as the property of prose, intensifies, the quasi-stanzaic structure of the early poems gives way to a different kind of structure, which, though less rhythmically uniform, remains tightly knit, and shows evidence of that rigorous 'pythagorean'[47] structure of the sonnet. The repetitions in 'Un hémisphère dans une chevelure' and 'L'Invitation au voyage' with their successive paragraphs beginning with 'Dans l'océan de ta chevelure', 'Dans les caresses de ta chevelure', 'Dans l'ardent foyer de ta chevelure', and 'Un pays de Cocagne', 'Un vrai pays de Cocagne', have an effect of harmony and incantation similar to that of a recurring refrain, which, as we have seen, may be at some slight variance with the tone of the poem; but this very obvious structure soon disappears. 'Un cheval de race' published in 1864, with its interplay of sentences about time and love — 'Le Temps et l'Amour l'ont marquée de leurs griffes', 'Le Temps n'a pu rompre l'harmonie pétillante de sa démarche [. . .] L'Amour n'a pas altéré

la suavité de son haleine d'enfant', 'Le Temps et l'Amour l'ont
vainement mordue à belles dents'—is the only one of the later poems
to employ anything like a stanzaic pattern of repetition, and this is
no doubt because it is a homage to Jeanne Duval, and a celebration
of her bizarre beauty which is suitable for a more lyrical treatment,
though the aesthetic of surprise is still present in the extraordinary
and contradictory metaphors and comparisons.[48] But the notion
of celebration is so rare in the prose poems as to be thought an
exception, barely compatible with the poet's evolving conception of
the genre. Examples of the kinds of structure which succeed the
stanzaic can be found in 'L'Étranger' with its question and answer
technique, and the repetition of the same words and the same form
of sentence, and much more characteristically in such short pieces as
'Le Désespoir de la vieille', 'Un plaisant', 'Chacun sa chimère', 'Le
Fou et la Vénus', 'Le Chien et le flacon', 'La Solitude', 'Les Fenêtres',
'Le Désir de peindre', 'Les Bienfaits de la lune', and 'Laquelle est la
vraie?'. These poems have a structure which, in a way vaguely
reminiscent of the sonnet or the 'rondel', is so geometrical as to be
immediately perceptible to the eye. Their effect is much stronger
when they are well set out typographically and are given a page to
themselves, instead of being divided between pages or even in the
middle of paragraphs. 'Le Désespoir de la vieille', whose paragraphs
in the original publication were separated by a double space, is one
of the finest examples:

La petite vieille ratatinée se sentit toute réjouie en voyant ce joli enfant
à qui chacun faisait fête, à qui tout le monde voulait plaire; ce joli être, si
fragile comme elle, la petite vieille, et, comme elle aussi, sans dents et sans
cheveux.

Et elle s'approcha de lui, voulant lui faire des risettes et des mines agréables.

Mais l'enfant épouvanté se débattait sous les caresses de la bonne femme
décrépite, et remplissait la maison de ses glapissements.

Alors la bonne vieille se retira dans sa solitude éternelle, et elle pleurait
dans un coin, se disant: — 'Ah! pour nous, malheureuses vieilles femelles,
l'âge est passé de plaire, même aux innocents; et nous faisons horreur aux
petits enfants que nous voulons aimer!'

The poem is made up of four short single-sentence paragraphs giving
in turn a description of the old woman and child, her approach to
the child, its fearful reaction, and finally her withdrawal, the strong
geometrical and logical structure of the piece being marked out by

the 'Et', 'Mais', and 'Alors' at the beginning of the paragraphs following the initial setting of the scene. One can see immediately what this technique owes to Bertrand whose *Gaspard de la nuit*[49] first gave Baudelaire the idea of trying to produce something similar, but one is even more aware of the profound differences. Baudelaire keeps something of Bertrand's couplets which are not based on the repetition of a 'refrain' as 'Un hémisphère dans une chevelure' was, at least to a limited extent; but he has replaced the Romantic and picturesque descriptions of old Dijon or Harlem by a stark and poignant scene with no concession to local colour, sentimentality, or nostalgia. Bertrand's descriptions have a static and timeless quality about them, while Baudelaire's poem is much more dynamic, the conjunctions giving the impression of movement, time, and the rapid unfolding of a very brief narration.

The sense of a progression and the tight-knit structure of these short pieces is accompanied by a strongly visual impression, as if one were looking at a picture. We have already seen that 'Le Désespoir de la vieille' is reminiscent of a genre painting; in addition, 'Un plaisant' could be a *croquis* by Guys or a caricature by Daumier, 'Chacun sa chimère' a Goya engraving, while the final paragraph of 'Laquelle est la vraie?' with the exasperated poet beating the ground so violently with his foot that his leg 's'est enfoncée jusqu'au genou dans la sépulture récente, et que, comme un loup pris au piège, je reste attaché, pour toujours peut-être, à la fosse de l'idéal' could be an allegorical representation of the poetic condition. The visual impact of these pieces is reinforced by their titles which have the pithiness and generality of captions for drawings or engravings. A similar visual effect is evident in parts of other poems, for example, the description of the 'vieux saltimbanque', of the father and son in 'Les Yeux des pauvres', the posture of the beseeching and adoring fool before the implacable statue of beauty in 'Le Fou et la Vénus', which probably comes from a pantomime by Deburau reconstructed in Marcel Carné's great film *Les Enfants du paradis*.[50] Such visual effects are to be expected in a volume which seeks to record the random and detached observations of the 'flâneur parisien' mingling with the crowd but avoiding any direct contact with other people.

The structure of the remaining pieces is much less obvious and rigorous, and has no formal resemblance whatsoever to a poem. Those which are based upon a 'soubresaut' have a clear turning-point,[51] most often in the middle of the poem, the shift from ideal

to spleen occurring in *Le Spleen de Paris* within the individual poems
rather than between groups of poems as is the tendency in *Les Fleurs
du Mal*. The 'essay' poems such as 'Les Bons Chiens', 'Les Veuves',
and, to a certain extent, 'Le Mauvais Vitrier' are decidedly digressive,
while the 'contes' such as 'Une mort héroïque', 'Mademoiselle
Bistouri', or 'Le Gâteau' are conducted with admirable simplicity
and economy. In this connection we might note the very rapid 'entrée
en matière', which is a feature of almost all of the poems. In 'La
Corde' the reader is plunged without introduction into the story
told by the poet's friend—'Les illusions, — me disait mon ami,—
sont aussi innombrables peut-être que les rapports des hommes entre
eux, ou des hommes avec les choses'—while in other poems the
establishing of the scene or situation and the description of individuals
is done with a very few, rapid strokes in a way, once again, which
is reminiscent of Constantin Guys in his *croquis*. The first two
paragraphs of 'Mademoiselle Bistouri' will suffice to illustrate these
two features:

> Comme j'arrivais à l'extrémité du faubourg, sous les éclairs du gaz, je sentis
> un bras qui se coulait doucement sous le mien, et j'entendis une voix qui
> me disait à l'oreille: 'Vous êtes médecin, monsieur?'
> Je regardai; c'était une grande fille, robuste, aux yeux très ouverts,
> légèrement fardée, les cheveux flottant au vent avec les brides de son bonnet.

The two single-sentence paragraphs provide a remarkably stark and
dramatic opening. In 'Les Sept Vieillards' where 'le spectre en plein
jour raccroche le passant', the poet is grasped by the bizarre and
the surreal with all the surprise and suddenness of a sexual advance.
The latent sexuality of the 'raccrochage' in the verse poem is here
rendered explicit and direct as the poet is approached by a real
whore with the unlikely question concerning his profession. Her
question is untypical and so are also the various elements in her
description which suggest health, innocence, and freedom rather than
prostitution, though retrospectively we come to understand that the
wide-open eyes denote the wildness and derangement of her mind.
With two brief and very dense sentences Baudelaire has projected
us right into a world of mystery and bizarreness.
A similar sense of immediacy at the beginning of a poem can be
conveyed by an exclamation ('Quelle admirable journée!'), by a
dogmatic statement of fact ('Fancioulle était un admirable bouffon'),
an injunction ('Il faut être toujours ivre'), or by an arresting paradox

('Elle est bien laide. Elle est délicieuse pourtant!'), so that although the genre of the prose poem permits, like the novel, of more detail than lyric poetry, since 'la lyre fuit volontiers tous les détails dont le roman se régale',[52] there is never any sense that the pieces which take the form of a narration are overburdened by superfluous comment or description.

Other pieces are conversations, dialogues, dreams, nightmares, or seeming fragments which might have been detached from a longer work; all of which shows that the prose poem, as Baudelaire practised it, covers a very wide range of sub-genres, which in turn are often mingled. Thus, 'Le Mauvais Vitrier' begins as a somewhat loose essay by an apparently detached observer of the folly of human conduct, which is then instanced by a short story or anecdote relating with great concision how the poet himself came on an occasion to break out into a paroxysm of frustration and violence against a poor seller of window panes. The almost too visible structure of some of the pieces is balanced by the throw-away casualness of such comments as 'J'ai oublié de vous dire que la distribution [. . .] est sans appel' in 'Les Dons des fées', or by the informal 'telegram' style of, for example, 'A une heure du matin'; 'avoir vu plusieurs hommes de lettres', 'avoir disputé généreusement contre le directeur d'une revue', 'avoir salué une vingtaine de personnes,' 'avoir refusé à un ami un service facile', etc.

The predominance of movement, narration, and exposition in the prose poems is, of course, an indication of their prosaic quality and their rejection of lyricism. This sense of movement which is an inherent factor in any story is quite different from the kind of movement which is to be found in many of the finest *Fleurs du Mal*, where it is resolved into immobility, but with no accompanying sense of stasis, emptiness, or death. The 'eurythmie' of 'L'Invitation au voyage', of the 'Infinis bercements du loisir embaumé', of the fascinating gait of the woman in 'Le Serpent qui danse', the rocking of ships at anchor, seems to enchant space and time and transport them to an absolute realm of perfection, in much the same way as for Valéry the dance is 'cette délivrance de notre corps tout entier possédé de l'esprit du mensonge, et de la musique qui est mensonge, et ivre de la négation de la nulle réalité'.[53] Such movement belongs to the timeless realm of being, whereas that of the stories and anecdotes of the 'flâneur parisien' belong to the hopelessly conting-ent real world of time and becoming. Similarly, Baudelaire's own predilection for a suggestive poetry made of 'sorcellerie évocatoire' would appear to put him in agreement with Sartre when he writes: 'Si le poète raconte, explique or enseigne, la poésie devient *prosaïque*, il a perdu la partie',[54] and would force him apparently to accept Max Jacob's strictures against the prose poems: 'La seule sympathie que je pourrais avoir pour ce littérateur descriptif de Baudelaire c'est qu'il y a eu là un effort d'invention. Tout ce qui est constatation, description, est antipoétique.'[55] These strictures are matched by Jean Cohen's analyses in *Structure du langage poétique* and *Le Haut Langage* of the difference between prose and poetry, and he concludes that whereas verse is an 'antiphrase' which aims at 'une homogénéité maxima entre les signifiants', prose seeks a maximum of differentiation.[56]

Whatever Baudelaire did intend and achieve in the prose poems, it was clearly something very different from what his comments in his correspondence seemed to indicate, something very different from the companion volume to *Les Fleurs du Mal*. Indeed, there seems to be a discrepancy between intention and achievement, and one is aware not only that his conception of the prose poem evolved considerably from his first experiments in the 1840s, but one suspects also that he was not totally in command of what he was doing and was not always sure of the direction he wished to take. It may well be that the difficulty of composition which he repeatedly mentions in his letters can in part be attributed to this uncertainty. He states in a letter of February 1861[57] and in the 'Dédicace' to Arsène Houssaye that the point of departure for the prose poems was Aloysius Bertrand's *Gaspard de la nuit*, so that his original intention was to create something analogous, and to apply to the description of modern life 'le procédé qu'il avait appliqué à la peinture de la vie ancienne'. In the event, he is aware 'que je faisais quelque chose de singulièrement différent', calling his creation an accident 'qui ne peut qu'humilier profondément un esprit qui regarde comme le plus grand honneur du poète d'accomplir *juste* ce qu'il a projeté de faire'. Even when allowance is made for false modesty and a playful irony towards Bertrand, the sense of an aesthetic accident is not entirely dispelled; and if the Symbolists' conception of the prose poem as 'une prose musicale, rythmée et assonancée, susceptible de se dissoudre en prose presque cursive ou de se resserrer jusqu'au vers, au contraire, par un jeu plus marqué d'accents et de sonorités',[58] owes much to Baudelaire's dream of a new poetic style as he defines it in the 'Dédicace', it owes very little, if anything, to his practice as it developed from the transpositions of the 1850s to the increasingly bitter and strident creations of the 1860s.

What he actually did achieve in *Le Spleen de Paris* is a puzzle to critics, as it was perhaps to the poet himself. It may well be that, as Huysmans has it, the prose poem in general terrifies the Homais of the world;[59] Baudelaire's have nothing to allay the fears of the critic who is aware of their dangers, complexities, and contradictions. Totally different from Bertrand, and certainly from Chateaubriand and Flaubert with their rising and falling cadences, their swelling and expansive ternary sentences, and the undulations of their reverie, Baudelaire has no real predecessors in the genre, nor has he any worthy successors. Rabbe, Lefèvre-Deumier, and Guérin produce brief nostalgic idylls within a cadre of Greek mythology, or prose meditations betraying an elegant world-weariness untouched by Baudelaire's bitterness and stridency;[60] and Rimbaud, or Char, for example, move towards the creation of entirely new rhythms, and dramatic compression and intensification of imagery; whereas Baudelaire stresses the prosaic quality of his pieces, so many of which are anecdotes, narrations of one kind or another, to such an extent that we wonder wherein the poetic element lies. Why call them poems at all? Has he perhaps failed in the impossible task of squaring the circle and making poetry out of the most naked and uncompromising prose?

Poe is, of course, relevant to the discussion, not only because 'Le Mauvais Vitrier', for example, shows something of Poe's imp of the perverse, but because Baudelaire was fascinated by Poe's short stories and admired them greatly. He liked them for their grotesque, macabre, and morbid subject-matter, concentrating on the horrors and infirmities of the mind; he also liked them for their shortness, for the same reasons, no doubt, as he preferred short poems to epic poems—not just because he was a 'paresseux nerveux' temperamentally incapable of the prolonged piece, but because he thought the epic did not produce 'cette excitation [. . .] cet *enlèvement* de l'âme',[61] and could not have unity and totality of effect, even though it might have unity of composition. Long poems are 'la ressource de ceux qui sont incapables d'en faire de courts'.[62] Similarly, he prefers the short story to the novel because it has the immense advantage over the novel of vast proportions that its brevity adds to the intensity of effect.[63] Like the short poem it produces the same unity of impression and totality of effect. Baudelaire's prose poems themselves, and the use of the adjective 'petits' in the title, reflect this aesthetic conviction that the poetic quality is related to the shortness of the pieces, though not in any mechanical way as Suzanne Bernard seems to suggest in her admirable *Le Poème en prose de Baudelaire jusqu'à nos jours*.[64] If that were the case, the eleven lines of 'Le Miroir' or the fifteen of 'Le Chien et le flacon' would be more poetic than the one hundred and thirty-one lines of 'Mademoiselle Bistouri', or the one hundred and sixty of 'Une mort héroïque', which is clearly not so. Suzanne Bernard's criterion is not, however, totally unfounded, and when she identifies as essential qualities of the prose poem 'gratuité', 'mystère', 'densité'[65] she comes much nearer to the truth. The criterion of poetic excellence should not just be the brevity together with that sense of the gratuitous fragment or throw-away piece, but, above all, its concentration and intensity, which, with only the appearance of a paradox, gives us a feeling of expansion, of a kind of 'psychedelic' multiplicity, not unlike the sudden illumination in Rimbaud, but on the level of subject-matter and thought rather than image. That Baudelaire was moving more and more towards a poetry of ideas, a poetry of 'signifiés' rather than 'signifiants', seems to have been perceived as early as the 1880s when Huysmans writes in *A rebours* :

De toutes les formes de la littérature, celle du poème en prose était la forme préférée de des Esseintes. Maniée par un alchimiste de génie, elle devait, suivant lui, renfermer, dans son petit volume, à l'état d'of meat, la puissance du roman dont elle supprimait les longueurs analytiques et les superfétations descriptives. Bien souvent, des Esseintes avait médité sur cet inquiétant problème, écrire un roman concentré en quelques phrases qui contiendraient le suc cohobé des centaines de pages toujours employées à établir le milieu, à dessiner les caractères, à entasser à l'appui les observations et les menus faits...

Le roman, ainsi conçu, ainsi condensé en une page ou deux, deviendrait une communion de pensée entre un magique écrivain et un idéal lecteur, une collaboration spirituelle consentie entre dix personnes supérieures éparses dans l'univers, une délectation offerte aux délicats, accessible à eux seuls.

En un mot, le poème en prose représentait, pour des Esseintes, le suc concret, l'osmazôme de la littérature, l'huile essentielle de l'art.

Cette succulence développée et réduite en une goutte, elle existait déjà chez Baudelaire, et aussi dans ces poèmes de Mallarmé qu'il humait avec une si profonde joie.[66]

Clearly some of Baudelaire's prose poems are more successful than others, but a fundamental criterion would be that of a hidden depth. The simplest pieces such as 'Le Désespoir de la vieille' contain only one idea which lurks beneath the surface; but as we read 'La Corde' and 'Mademoiselle Bistouri' and ponder the relationship of art to experience, of love to surgery, prostitution to innocence, madness to kindness, or as we meditate on the identity of the cruel prince and the mime, and the links between art, buffoonery, violence, and death in 'Une mort héroïque', these stories fascinate with a meaning or meanings which go far beyond their literal sense. They have something of the elliptic allegories of Kafka, or of the mystery and density of Borges's fictions, and before such narrations we can adopt the same criterion as Baudelaire himself for judging the excellence of a painting: 'Il m'arrivera souvent d'apprécier un tableau uniquement par la somme d'idées ou de rêveries qu'il apportera dans mon esprit.'[67] Such pieces might be said to be as successful 'poetically' as 'La Chevelure' or 'Parfum exotique', since the story they relate has a power and a 'rayonnement' analogous to those of the images in the finest verse poems. In the extreme concentration of their thought they have a similar power to fascinate the mind, and a quality reminiscent of the 'expansion des choses infinies' which is celebrated in 'Correspondances', and that property of all great art which is to 'faire rêver'.[68]

A second criterion of poetic excellence, which is linked to that sense of moral anarchy at the heart of things which we witnessed in Chapter II, might be thought to be the extent to which the poet creates in the prose poems a universe which is predominantly violent and surreal. It has on occasion been affirmed that the prose poems are marked by a realism of detail and description which provides a compelling evocation of the life in the modern capital. But very few of the poems, if indeed any, are in fact descriptions of the real world and nothing more, and those which come nearest to such a definition tend to be among the least interesting in the collection, for example 'Le Chien et le flacon', in spite (or possibly because) of its obvious symbolism. Some are placed resolutely within a fantasy or dream world, such as 'Les Dons des fées', 'Les Tentations', 'Chacun sa chimère', and 'L'Invitation au voyage', and 'Un hémisphère dans une chevelure'. But among the most compelling are those in which Baudelaire mingles and fuses the real with the imaginary, so that the poems take on the properties of a hallucination in which 'la profondeur de la vie'[69] is revealed at its most intense and most disturbing. They are similar to 'Les Sept Vieillards' in *Les Fleurs du Mal* where the poet's baleful vision of the seven old men becomes an incomprehensible and nightmarish hallucination:

> Vainement ma raison voulait prendre la barre;
> La tempête en jouant déroutait ses efforts,
> Et mon âme dansait, dansait, vieille gabarre
> Sans mâts, sur une mer monstrueuse et sans bords!

Often the passage from the real to the surreal is brought about through the heightening and intensification of the power and vitality of a street scene, as, for example, in the 'explosion' of the New Year in 'Un plaisant':

> C'était l'explosion du nouvel an: chaos de boue et de neige, traversé de mille carosses, étincelant de joujoux et de bonbons, grouillant de cupidités et de désespoirs, délire officiel d'une grande ville fait pour troubler le cerveau du solitaire le plus fort.

At the beginning of this anecdote we are plunged into a 'real' world which threatens to return to chaos, and where men appear to have gone mad. Similarly, but more acutely, in 'Le Vieux Saltimbanque' we have the evocation of the vitality and stridency of the fair: 'Partout s'étalait, se répandait, s'ébaudissait le peuple en vacances.' There are the 'baraques' which 'piaillaient, beuglaient, hurlaient'. 'C'était un mélange de cris, de détonations de cuivre et d'explosions de fusées.' We are told that 'Tout n'était que lumière, poussière, cris, joie, tumulte'. In this 'real' world the mind is bombarded with many new and unusual happenings and sensations of all kinds, so that it takes on the terrifying unreality of a nightmare in which reason has lost its grip and is numbed and bewildered by the assault upon the senses. Against such a reality which has returned to chaos and is engulfed in madness, the figure of the Saltimbanque stands out with greater poignancy, like Awareness itself isolated amidst the unthinking absurdity and primitive clamour of the passions and the senses.

There are other transitions from the real world which are apparently calmer, as, for example, in 'Le Crépuscule du soir':

> Le jour tombe. Un grand apaisement se fait dans les pauvres esprits fatigués du labeur de la journée; et leurs pensées prennent maintenant les couleurs tendres et indécises du crépuscule.
> Cependant du haut de la montagne arrive à mon balcon, à travers les nues transparentes du soir, un grand hurlement, composé d'une foule de cris

discordants, que l'espace transforme en une lugubre harmonie, comme celle de la marée qui monte ou d'une tempête qui s'éveille.

The references to the peace of evening, to the mountain top, and to the transparent clouds prepare us for the relaxation and the 'vague-à-l'âme' of a Lamartinian meditation, but gradually we find ourselves in another world where the complaint of the wretched is made audible, and where a 'lugubre harmonie' is made out of what is discordant, a harmony which threatens to return to an even greater chaos than before, like the uneasy peace before the unleashing of a storm. We start in one mode of perception and end in another, where the abstract is made concrete, and where harmony and discordance appear, momentarily at least, reconciled.

Such an example might be said to be half-way between the discordant clamour and the outburst of vitality we have witnessed in the fair or in the Paris street scene and that silent orgy of light and energy which is to be found in 'Le Fou et la Vénus'. We start in a real park, but immediately the heightened presence of light, and indeed of all things, gives to it the intensity it can only have in certain dreams or states of hallucination, where a sense of menace is present together with one of tranquillity:

> Quelle admirable journée! Le vaste parc se pâme sous l'œil brûlant du soleil, comme la jeunesse sous la domination de l'Amour.
> L'extase universelle des choses ne s'exprime par aucun bruit; les eaux elles-mêmes sont comme endormies. Bien différente des fêtes humaines, c'est ici une orgie silencieuse.
> On dirait qu'une lumière toujours croissante fait de plus en plus étinceler les objets; que les fleurs excitées brûlent du désir de rivaliser avec l'azur du ciel par l'énergie de leurs couleurs, et que la chaleur, rendant visibles les parfums, les fait monter vers l'astre comme des fumées.

It is as if nature itself here had taken on the same fascinating quality, and were endowed with the same intense presence, as the visions of *Paradis artificiels*[70] and of 'La Chambre double', as if it had a life and a being of its own totally independent of human thought and action, and this feeling is made all the more powerful and disquieting by the detachment of the figure of the Fool absorbed in his worship of the implacable and immortal goddess Venus. Such a hyperbolic description with its increasing intensity is at once ecstatic and frightening, in much the same way as Hugo's descriptions fill us with awe before a numinous world where 'tout est plein d'âmes'.[71] Once again, as in 'Le Vieux Saltimbanque', we feel the rational mind losing its grip as the surreal invades the real. Such a vision, with its suggestion of the elevation of all things towards the light and the spiritual world, threatens to degenerate into a nightmare, and instead of a beatific vision we have a terrifying glimpse, albeit momentary, of the horrific orgy of the natural world described by Sartre in *La Nausée*, of the hellish otherness of things which threaten to violate and engulf the mind. A similar disquiet at the exuberance of nature is evident in 'Le Tir et le cimetière' where 'le soleil ivre se vautrait tout de son long sur un tapis de fleurs magnifiques engraissées par la destruction'. It is rendered all the more threatening by the parallel which is established between the clamour of nature and that of the unthinking public at the firing range.

In this connection it is instructive to notice the frequency and the particular use of the word 'explosion' in some of the prose poems, signifying not so much an outburst of creative activity as the subjection of the poet to a sensory experience in which the controlling factors of reason and awareness are lost: in 'Un plaisant', 'C'était l'explosion du nouvel an'; in 'Le Désir de peindre' there is an 'explosion dans les ténèbres' in the eyes of the poet's mistress, and in 'Une mort héroïque' the admiring crowd breaks out into 'explosions de la joie et de l'admiration' which have the power and energy of a continuous thunder. In all these explosions there is some threat which is more or less explicit, even in those which seem to reach a reconciliation between violence and tranquillity. In 'Le Désir de peindre', for example, we are given a sense of calm by the comparison of the light in his mistress's eyes with that of the moon, until we are told that it is not the white moon of idylls, but the moon which has been 'arrachée du ciel, vaincue et révoltée, que les Sorcières thessaliennes contraignent durement à danser sur l'herbe terrifiée'. The sense of calm is soon dispersed by the suggestion of some kind of cosmic disaster in which the world is given over to the forces of chaos and unreason.

Closely linked with these violent outbursts are those pieces which describe 'les soubresauts de la conscience', these sudden changes of mood or feeling which always move in *Le Spleen de Paris* from the serene, ecstatic, and ideal towards anguish, torment, and a debased reality. The most striking examples of this are where the change of mood to its opposite, marked by expressions such as 'mais', 'toutefois', 'bref', 'tout à coup', takes place in the middle of a piece, creating an impression of chaotic discontinuity. In 'La Chambre double', for example, we witness the fall from a fascinated, timeless, and beatific vision which transforms the ordinary surroundings of the poet as if childhood had been found again by chance, back into the sordid reality of his hotel room with its 'meubles sots, poudreux, écornés; la cheminée sans flamme et sans braise, souillée de crachats; les tristes fenêtres où la pluie a tracé des sillons dans la poussière'. The heavy knock which resounds on the door brings the importunate reality of bailiff, concubine, or publisher's 'saute-ruisseau' demanding copy, and gone is the 'chambre spirituelle', the dream of eternity, the ideal woman, the 'rêve de volupté pendant une éclipse'. Similarly in 'La Soupe et les nuages' the poet's vague musing is cruelly interrupted by the raucous voice of his mistress, roughened by cheap spirits, telling him to get on with his soup, and in 'Le *Confiteor* de l'artiste' the movement from one extreme to its opposite is all the more intense and striking for being unexpected and unmotivated. No reason is given for the change from a serene contemplation of sea and sky, in which the poet identifies himself in a quasi-pantheistic fashion with the immensity of nature, to the violent, anguished, and staccato outcry: 'Et maintenant la profondeur du ciel me consterne; sa limpidité m'exaspère. L'insensibilité de la mer, l'immuabilité du spectacle me révoltent.' The fault is not as in 'La Chambre double' with the intrusion of an importunate and philistine outside world; the fault, as we have seen, lies within the poet himself whose nerves seem unable to tolerate the tension of the aesthetic experience. It is important to stress that in these 'soubresauts de la conscience' the movement is always from ideal to spleen; the curve of the pieces never goes in the opposite direction,[72] which again contributes to the poet's doubts about the status of art and of the artist, creating ultimately in 'Le *Confiteor*', as in 'Chacun sa chimère', a sense of lassitude, despair, and indifference, culminating in the depressing maxim that 'l'étude du beau est un duel où l'artiste crie de frayeur avant d'être vaincu'.

Other kinds of 'soubresaut' are much less dramatic since they take place within a section of a poem whose tone is more or less even. They may take the form of a sudden change in linguistic register as when the slang expression 'mirettes' is used in the first, ecstatic, part of 'La Chambre double' to describe the eyes of the ideal Sylphide, or they may be in the form of an oxymoron where the contradiction takes place within a whole sentence or in a phrase such as 'C'est le plus lourd, le plus sot et le plus célèbre de tous mes auteurs', or 'sainte prostitution', 'soleil noir', 'monstres innocents', 'infatigable mélancolie'. As many of the titles indicate—'Le Fou et la Vénus', 'La Soupe et les nuages', 'Assommons les pauvres!'—such a technique is essential to Baudelaire's aesthetic of the prose poem, its function being a generalized sense of unease, dissonance, and threatened chaos and violence.

The various kinds of humour one finds in the prose poems are clearly very closely linked to such an aesthetic, the most basic being the use of a gross and vulgar vocabulary which one would not expect to find in a serious work of poetry. Hugo had already put 'le bonnet rouge' on the dictionary of poetic language with the introduction of technical terms and such daring intrusions as 'vache', 'bateau', 'poire', and 'mâchoire';[73] but the prose poems go much further, with references to spit, soot, excrement, rats, 'sauteuses', soup, henpecked husbands, broken teeth, blacked eyes, together with a variety of oaths and expletives. Some expressions could come only from the totally uneducated like 'Vénustre' for Vénus, while others, though not slang or uneducated, have at once a comic and a conversational tonality, as when in 'Les Dons des fées' the fairies are described as being 'aussi *ahuries* (my italics) que des ministres un jour d'audience'. By contrast, there is the humour of overstatement which consists in dignifying an essentially base or trivial object with a pseudo-scientific terminology, as when children in 'Déjà!' are referred to as 'progéniture criarde', or a mistress[74] is called a '*monstre polyphage*'. A variation on this kind of humour is the disporportionate comparison, as, for example, when the ticket-collectors at the theatre appear to the timid would-be spectator as terrifying as the gods of the underworld, Minos, Aeacus, and Rhadamanthus. There is the discreet irony, which talks of the regimental music in 'Les Veuves' which 'gratifie le peuple parisien', which refers to the murder of the perfect mistress as 'une action rigoureuse', or which plays down the violence in 'Le Mauvais Vitrier' by calling it 'une plaisanterie nerveuse', all of which contrasts with the strident, slapstick humour of 'La Femme sauvage'. Finally, there are the wilfully debilitated puns in 'Une mort héroïque', where the cruel prince wishes to make 'une expérience physiologique d'un intérêt *capital*', or where the Devil in 'Le Joueur généreux' wishes the poet to have a happy memory of him and 'prouver que Moi, dont on dit tant de mal, je suis quelquefois *bon diable*, pour me servir d'une de vos locutions vulgaires'.

The significance of humour in the prose poems becomes much more apparent in the light of his theory of laughter in *De l'essence du rire*. In that essay he claims he is not interested in joviality or the laughter of the child, which is likened to the spontaneous blossoming of a flower: 'C'est la joie de recevoir, la joie de respirer, la joie de s'ouvrir, la joie de contempler, de vivre, de grandir.'[75] He more or less begins his study by attributing to Joseph de Maistre, the notorious exponent of the doctrine of original sin who, Baudelaire claimed, taught him to think, the aphorism 'Le Sage ne rit qu'en tremblant' (in fact the idea is Bossuet's).[76] Baudelaire's theory is that the comic is linked to the idea of original sin, that it is linked, consequently, to the doctrine of the fall of man, 'à l'accident d'une chute ancienne, d'une dégradation physique et morale'.[77] He would, no doubt, also have agreed with Bergson[78] that the comic comes from a stilling of the emotions, and from a purely intellectual apprehension of a situation. Indeed, Baudelaire says that the comic must have been one of the seeds of the original forbidden fruit, and that laughter comes from the idea of one's superiority, 'Idée satanique s'il en fut jamais!'[79] He goes on to examine the satanic laugh of the villain in romantic novels and melodrama, particularly of Maturin's Melmoth, whose laughter is seen to spring from his dual nature, that is to say from his feeling of superiority over other men, and from his infinite vileness and baseness in relationship to absolute good and justice. In other words, Baudelaire is saying that humour is something essentially human and essentially contradictory, the sign at one and the same time of an infinite grandeur and an infinite 'misère'.

The relevance of this theory to such prose poems as 'Le Joueur généreux' and, in particular, 'Une mort héroïque' should be immediately obvious; for one can detect in the stories a belief not in an order of beauty, truth, and goodness, but of ugliness, anarchy, and injustice. The superiority of the prince is in his lucidity, in his satanic cynicism, and his apprehension of the ultimately unsatisfactory nature of art itself, that is, in the acceptance and cultivation of his fallen condition. Laughter comes, in short, from a recognition of our aspiration towards the ideal, and of the impossibility of attaining it. It is, consequently, never far away from the famous 'rire en pleurs' of Villon, which is developed in the nineteenth-century cult of the buffoon and the pierrot. Like spleen and ideal, 'l'extase de la vie et l'horreur de la vie', God and Satan, heaven and hell, vaporization and centralization, the comic and the tragic, laughter and tears in Baudelaire are not so much contradictory as complementary.

André Breton is certainly right to equate Baudelaire's humour with his 'dandysme',[80] which is the cult of the artificial in one's person, the rejection of the natural because of its laxity, stupidity, and mindlessness. The cult of the artificial and of the beautiful leads eventually to a kind of asceticism, to a rejection of passion and sentiment, and to the cultivation of an 'air froid' and the 'inébranlable résolution de ne pas être ému'.[81] In his protest against nature the dandy is unmoved, impassive, ascetic, almost saint-like in his stoicism. But it is important that Baudelaire's 'dandysme', his mystifications, his 'plaisir aristocratique de déplaire'[82] are all manifestations of the deeper and fundamental conviction of original sin.

The most original, and the most disturbing, kind of humour in the prose poems is to be found in that extreme exaggeration of 'le rire en pleurs' which Breton called black humour. There are several examples of it in the collection, of varying intensity and all related in one way or another to an outburst of violence, whether it be the controlled violence of 'le galant tireur' who kills his wife in effigy, the discreet violence of the 'désabusé' rake who alludes with impeccable good taste and understatement to his drowning of his perfect mistress, or that overt violence of the poet who beats up the poor man who asks for alms. The best and most notorious example is without doubt 'Le Mauvais Vitrier' which is also among the most perfect in the collection. From his sixth-floor garret the poet sees a poor 'vitrier' whose piercing and discordant cry rises up to him through the muggy Paris atmosphere. Having called him up, he gruffly dismisses him for not having rose-coloured panes through which to see 'la vie en beau'. When the poor man reaches the street again, the poet throws a flowerpot down at him, smashing all his panes, and depriving him and his family of the proceeds of his day's labour.

Much has been written about this poem, which can be offensive to those who prefer a literature of 'bons sentiments'. No doubt it reflects Baudelaire's desire to mystify and to cause displeasure, but what is significant and blackly humorous is the sudden change from contemplation and lethargy on the part of the poet to violent, hysterical, satanic, and apparently unmotivated action. In such moments, as in the paintings of Goya whom he admired, and as in the poems of Lautréamont whom he prefigures, it is as if the poet were taking the side of the dark, ugly, and arbitrary powers which seem to govern our world, and thereby he gives us a deeper insight into our condition, showing at the same time the inadequacies of a facile and unthinking humanism. This kind of black humour would seem, therefore, to have a similar function in the prose poems to the one defined by Michel Carrouges in his book on Surrealism:[83] 'L'humour noir est un rire insultant qui part du fond du moi révolté, provoque et défie l'opinion publique et le fatum cosmique'. Furthermore, like sex, wine, or any other 'paradis artificiel', it is profoundly satisfying, at least momentarily, since it has the power to circumvent spleen, that pathological apprehension of our fallen condition. This is clearly the meaning of the poet's exultant cry at the end of the piece: 'qu'importe l'éternité de la damnation à qui a trouvé dans une seconde l'infini de la jouissance?'

It is not clear from his writings on the essence of laughter and on French and foreign caricaturists how Baudelaire would have classified the kind of humour exemplified in 'Le Mauvais Vitrier'. On the one hand, it has in an exaggerated form something of the diabolical laugh of Melmoth, and the accompanying sense of original sin and of fallen humanity; on the other hand, paradoxically, it seems to have the violence, the 'vertige de l'hyperbole', and 'quelque chose de terrible et d'irrésistible'[84] which Baudelaire recognizes as the distinctive signs of the grotesque and the 'comique absolu', which he is at pains to distinguish from the much less dramatic 'rire significatif'.[85] That Baudelaire associates certain kinds of humour with violence is borne out by his essays on the caricaturists where he writes of the 'explosion', the 'dégagement'[86] of the comic, and the way it forces us into another world: the caricature of the 1830 Revolution is a 'tohu-bohu, un capharnaüm, une prodigieuse comédie satanique, tantôt bouffonne, tantôt sanglante';[87] the caricatures of Cruikshank show 'la violence extravagante du geste et du mouvement, et l'explosion dans l'expression',[88] while Goya portrays 'toutes les hyperboles de l'hallucination', 'un échantillon du chaos'.[89]

At all events, violence, hallucination, and chaos are all associated by Baudelaire with certain kinds of humour and caricature, and all are powerful ingredients of *Le Spleen de Paris*, pointing to a world where order and reason have been replaced by anarchy and madness in both the moral and physical spheres. However, it may be justly asked why violence, gratuitousness, and chaos should be equated with the poetic. It would appear that what Baudelaire achieved in many of the prose poems, and may well have had in mind as a partially conceived intention, was a kind of poetry of disharmony, an intoxication not with things having endless resonance and expansiveness, but with what might be called an 'ivresse de l'absurde', an ecstasy made not of a spiritual elevation in which all things flow together 'dans une ténébreuse et profonde unité, / Vaste comme la nuit et comme la clarté', but as Malraux said in a very different context, 'une extase vers le bas',[90] an ecstasy at the horrific and gratuitous presence of things, which refuse to submit to the analyses and categories of the mind, and which seem to escape from the domain of language and logical discourse. Here it must be stressed that the metaphors and similes of the prose poems do not suggest that unified world, that 'coincidentia oppositorum', which Léon Cellier claimed is the result of Baudelaire's use of oxymoron in *Les Fleurs du Mal*: 'le poète est celui qui en usant de l'antithèse et de l'oxymoron, passe d'un univers tragique à un paradis, de la dualité à l'unité'.[91] As we glimpsed in discussing 'L'Invitation au voyage' and 'Un hémisphère dans une chevelure', the images in the prose poems are frequently disjunctive rather than conjunctive; oxymoron does not overcome opposites but leaves them in the disharmony and incompatibility of mere juxtaposition. The arabesque line, 'la plus spiritualiste',[92] gives way to the 'ligne brisée', and the prose poems could indeed be taken for the *locus classicus* of the way in which Analogy, so much prized by Romantics and Symbolists,[93] is subverted by irony, an irony which either exaggerates a figure or presents it in too literal a manner. To demand rose-coloured window panes in order to see 'la vie en beau' is so insanely literal as to destroy the figure, and with it the prestige of the notion of the poet as 'voyant', endowed with a special vision which can transform the fallen world into a paradise regained. Similarly, at the end of 'Laquelle est la vraie?' the posture of the poet with his leg sunk up to the knee in the recently dug grave of his beloved Bénédicta, so that like a wolf caught in a trap he remains 'attaché, pour toujours peut-être, à la fosse de l'idéal', is highly significant, not just because it represents his despair concerning the ideal, but because this meaning has been incorporated in an allegorical figure so exaggerated and hyperbolic as to become a caricature of figurality itself.[94] The highest flights of lyricism in *Les Fleurs du Mal* point to another order of things, a vision of oneness where contradiction is overcome, where time and separation no longer prevail, and where analysis is replaced by the perceptions of a superior faculty. The 'lyricism' of the prose poems is at the opposite pole, describing an 'ecstasy' before the irrational in which mere juxtaposition has stunned and paralysed the mind into a sense of infernal stasis and timelessness.

Notes

Chapter I

References are to the *Œuvres complètes* (Paris, Gallimard, Bibliothèque de la Pléiade, i, 1975, ii, 1976, ed. Cl. Pichois) and to *Correspondance* i and ii (Bibliothèque de la Pléiade, 1973, ed. Cl. Pichois).

1. *Corr.* ii, 627.
2. Ibid., 271. See also pp. 339, 523, 566, 572.
3. Ibid., 615.
4. 'J'ai essayé d'enfermer là-dedans toute l'amertume et toute la mauvaise humeur dont je suis plein.' (ibid., 339.)
5. 'Tout enfant, j'ai senti dans mon cœur deux sentiments contradictoires, l'horreur de la vie et l'extase de la vie.' (i. 703.)
6. *Corr.* ii. 473.
7. '. . . je suis toujours préoccupé de l'horreur de la plaquette' (*Corr.* i. 376.)
8. 'Les artistes qui voient les lignes sous le luxe et l'efflorescence de la couleur percevront très bien qu'il y a ici *une architecture secrète*, un plan calculé par le poète, méditatif et volontaire.' (i. 1196.) The whole of Barbey's article is reproduced in the Pichois edition.
9. See D. J. Mossop, *Baudelaire's Tragic Hero*, London, Oxford University Press, 1961.
10. *Corr.* ii. 196. See ibid., p. 199, where Baudelaire talks of the second edition of *Les Fleurs du Mal*, 'refondue et augmentée de trente-cinq morceaux nouveaux adaptés au cadre général'. Also, 'Je suis un de ceux (et nous sommes bien rares) qui croient que toute composition littéraire, même critique, doit être faite et manœuvrée en vue d'un dénouement.' (*Corr.* i. 538.)
11. See M. A. Ruff, *Baudelaire*, Paris, Hatier, 1966, pp. 105–6; 'l'édition de 1857 est centrée tout entière sur le destin du poète, plutôt que de l'homme en général, comme le marque le sonnet qui clôt le volume sur *La Mort des artistes*.'
12. *Corr.* ii. 141.
13. See i. 682–3: 'Il y a dans tout homme, à toute heure, deux postulations simultanées, l'une vers Dieu, l'autre vers Satan. L'invocation à Dieu, ou spiritualité, est un désir de monter en grade; celle de Satan, ou animalité, est une joie de descendre.'
14. Leo Bersani, *Baudelaire and Freud*, Berkeley, University of California Press, 1977, p. 22.

15 Ibid., p. 2.
16 Laforgue, *Poésies complètes*, ed. Pascal Pia, Paris, 'Livre de poche', 1970, p. 84.
17 No matter how uncertain Baudelaire's attitudes towards Christianity were, he seems to have remained faithful to the notions of original sin and the mind–body duality.
18 i. 275. See also i. 365 where it appears that Baudelaire at one time thought of giving the volume the title 'Les 66' or '666' or even '6666', six having associations with the Devil. See Rev. 13: 18.
19. 'Dans *Le Spleen de Paris*, il y aura cent morceaux — il en manque encore trente.' (*Corr.* ii. 324.)
20. i. 366–74.
21. *Corr.* ii. 583. My italics.
22. i. 428.
23. Ibid.
24. P. Bourget, *Essais de psychologie contemporaine*, Paris, Lemerre, 1890, i. p. 25.
25. Writing of Aloysius Bertrand's *Gaspard de la nuit*, Baudelaire claims that with the prose poems the idea came to him 'de tenter quelque chose d'analogue, et d'appliquer à la description de la vie moderne, ou plutôt d'*une* vie moderne et plus abstraite, le procédé qu'il avait appliqué à la peinture de la vie ancienne, si étrangement pittoresque' (i. 275).
26. *Petits Poëmes en prose*, édition critique par Robert Kopp, Paris, Corti, 1969, p. 185. The passage in question is in ii, 666.
27. G. Bachelard, *L'Air et les songes*, Paris, Corti, 1950, p. 222.
28. *Le Spleen de Paris*, édition de H. Lemaître, Paris, Garnier, 1962, p. 13. The passage in question is in ii. 438–9.
29. ii. 653. See also *Corr.* i. 676: 'Avez-vous observé qu'un morceau de ciel, aperçu par un soupirail, ou entre deux cheminées, deux rochers, ou par une arcade, etc., donnait une idée plus profonde de l'infini que le grand panorama vu du haut d'une montagne?'
30. See 'Le Reniement de saint Pierre'.
31. The futility of such a contemplation is evident in the last sentence of 'Le Port': 'Et puis, surtout, il y a une sorte de plaisir mystérieux et aristocratique pour celui qui n'a plus ni curiosité ni ambition, à contempler, couché dans le belvédère ou accoudé sur le môle, tous ces mouvements de ceux qui partent et de ceux qui reviennent, de ceux qui ont encore la force de vouloir, le désir de voyager ou de s'enrichir.'
    David Scott is right to draw attention to the fragmentary nature of this piece and of 'Déjà!' and 'Any where out of this world'—'all of which reflect different aspects of the voyage theme but none of which exudes that self-confident lyricism so typical of Baudelaire's verse poems of the 1850s of which "Le Voyage" was one of the last great examples' (*Baudelaire: La Fanfarlo and 'Le Spleen de Paris'*, London, Grant and Cutler, 1984, p. 66).

32. See my 'Baudelaire, Manet, et "La Corde" ', *Bulletin baudelairien*, xix, no. 1 (1984), 7–11, for a fuller discussion of the poem.
33. See also Ch. II, p. 50. In an earlier version published in *L'Artiste* in Nov. 1864 this moral lesson was clearly spelled out, rather than suggested, in a final paragraph which Baudelaire rightly suppressed: 'Parbleu! — répondis-je à mon ami, — un mètre de corde de pendu, à cent francs le décimètre, l'un dans l'autre, chacun payant selon ses moyens, cela fait mille francs, un réel, un efficace soulagement pour cette pauvre mère!' (i. 1339.)
34. On 7 Feb. 1864.
35. Ph. Rebeyrol, 'Baudelaire et Manet', *Les Temps modernes*, no. 48, Oct. 1949, pp. 707–25, and Lois Boe Hyslop, *Baudelaire, Man of his Time*, London and New Haven, Yale, University Press, 1980, pp. 47–61.
36. *Corr.* ii. 497. Baudelaire's italics.
37. See *Salon de 1846*, ch. II, and *Le Peintre de la vie moderne*, V.
38. 'L'Enfant aux cerises' (1858–9) is an oil painting, 'Le Garçon et le chien' (1861) is an engraving. See i. 1339.
39. Proust, *A la recherche du temps perdu*, Paris, Gallimard, 1954, iii. 723.
40. J. Prévost, *Baudelaire*, Paris, Mercure de France, 1953, p. 36, and Kopp, ed. cit., p. 346.
41. R. Klein, ' "Bénédiction" | "Perte d'auréole": Parables of Interpretation', *Modern Language Notes*, lxxxv, no. 4, May 1970, p. 527.
42. Likewise the poet in 'Bénédiction' who 'joue avec le vent, cause avec le nuage' is ridiculed in 'La Béatrice', where he appears as a caricature and as a 'Histrion en vacances'.
43. E. Welsford, *The Fool: His Social and Literary History*, London, Faber, 1935. See also Louisa E. Jones, *Sad Clowns and Pale Pierrots: Literature and the Popular Comic Arts in 19th-Century France*, Lexington, French Forum, 1984.
44. Ch. Mauron, *Le Dernier Baudelaire*, Paris, Corti, 1966, p. 136.
45. See 'Vagabonds' in *Illuminations*.
46. ii. 650. Cf. ibid., p. 784.
47. As in Marcel Carné's film *Les Enfants du paradis* which recreated 'Marchand d'habits' as described by Gautier in *Souvenirs de théâtre*, Paris, Charpentier, 1883, pp. 55–67.
48. H. Lemaître, ed. cit., p. 35, thinks the allegory becomes autobiographical, uniting two kinds of inferiority complex: 'celui de l'homme devant la femme et celui du poète devant son idéal'.
49. Jean Starobinski, *Portrait de l'artiste en saltimbanque*, Geneva, Skira, 1970, and 'Sur quelques répondants allégoriques du poète', *Revue d'histoire littéraire de la France*, lxvii, Apr.–June 1967, pp. 402–12; Ch. Mauron, op. cit.; Ross Chambers, ' "L'art sublime du comédien" ou le regardant regardé', *Saggi e ricerche di letteratura francese*, xi, 1971, pp. 189–260.
50. i. 580.
51. i. 702.

52. 'Victor Hugo était, dès le principe, l'homme le mieux doué, le plus visiblement élu pour exprimer par la poésie ce que j'appellerai le *mystère de la vie*'. (ii. 131.)
53. ii. 690.
54. 'Moesta et errabunda', line 21.
55. ii. 540–1.
56. ii. 535.
57. Cf. Flaubert, 'Je veux qu'il y ait une amertume à tout, un éternel coup de sifflet au milieu de nos triomphes, et que la désolation même soit dans l'enthousiasme' (*Corr.*, Paris, Conard, iii. 137).
58. Cf. also 'Les Vocations', where the third little boy seemed to be crowned by 'une auréole sulfureuse de passion'.
59. 'Or, la grande poésie est essentiellement *bête*, elle *croit*, et c'est ce qui fait sa gloire et sa force.' (ii. 11.)
60. ii. 629
61. As in, for example, 'Le Jeu'.
62. La Rochefoucauld, *Maximes*, no. 26.
63. Art. cit.
64. For Baudelaire's condemnation of eclecticism, see ii. 472–4.
65. Op. cit., ch. V.
66. T. S. Eliot in his essay 'Hamlet' of 1919.
67.   Ruines! ma famille! ô cerveaux congénères!
           Je vous fais chaque soir un solennel adieu!
                                       (lines 81–2.)
68. In 'Les Veuves' Baudelaire says of public gardens that 'ces retraites ombreuses sont les rendez-vous des éclopés de la vie'.
69. 'Le Jeu'.
70. See Alison Fairlie, *Imagination and Language: Collected Essays on Constant, Baudelaire, Nerval and Flaubert*, Cambridge University Press, 1981, pp. 173–4: 'Dans "Les Vocations", à travers les rêves de quatre enfants, Baudelaire évoque quatre aspects de la vision de l'artiste: — mimétique, mystique, sensuelle, imaginative.'
71. 'Je lis dans un singulier philosophe quelques lignes qui me font rêver à l'art des grands acteurs:
    "Quand je veux savoir jusqu'à quel point quelqu'un est circonspect ou stupide, jusqu'à quel point il est bon ou méchant, ou quelles sont actuellement ses pensées, je compose mon visage d'après le sien, aussi exactement que possible, et j'attends alors pour savoir quels pensers ou quels sentiments naîtront dans mon esprit ou dans mon cœur, comme pour s'appareiller et correspondre avec ma physionomie."
    Et quand le grand acteur, nourri de son rôle, habillé, grimé, se trouve en face de son miroir, horrible ou charmant, séduisant ou répulsif, et qu'il y contemple cette nouvelle personnalité qui doit devenir la sienne pendant quelques heures, il tire de cette analyse un nouveau parachèvement, une espèce de magnétisme de récurrence.' (ii. 65.)

72. ii. 607.
73. ii. 691–2. See also in connection with Poe ii. 277: *'L'Homme des foules se plonge sans cesse au sein de la foule; il nage avec délices dans l'océan humain.'*
74. 'Le *Confiteor* de l'artiste'.
75. Walter Benjamin, *Charles Baudelaire: A Lyric Poet in the Era of High Capitalism*, London, NLB, 1973, p. 125.
76. i. 692. For a discussion of the notion of 'prostitution', see *Journaux intimes*, ed. Crépet et Blin, Paris, Corti, 1949, pp. 204 ff.
77. i. 649.
78. Ibid.
79. Flaubert, *Corr.* v. 257.
80. i. 676
81. Cf. 'L'Homme et la mer'.
82. i. 700.
83. Cf. 'Le Chien et le flacon'.
84. See Cl. Pichois's comments on Baudelaire's inability to 'sortir de lui-même, and his 'incapacité à être autre et à être autrui' (i. 1403).
85. Such an attitude inevitably casts some doubt on Baudelaire's proud claim in a letter to his mother: 'Le propre des vrais poètes — pardonnez-moi cette petite bouffée d'orgueil, c'est le seul qui me soit permis — est de savoir sortir d'eux-mêmes, et comprendre une tout autre nature.' (*Corr.* i. 334.)
86. Lemaître, ed. cit., p. xlviii.
87. B. Johnson, *Défigurations du langage poétique*, Paris, Flammarion, 1978, p. 65.
88. One wonders whether, by shifting the emphasis away from the 'volonté/fantaisie' duality which is the main theme of the poem towards the duality of unity and variety, Barbara Johnson has not brought about a blurring of focus. As the passage she quotes shows very clearly, the duality concerns 'unité de but' and 'variété des moyens'.
89. See Melvin Zimmerman, 'La Genèse du symbole du thyrse chez Baudelaire', *Bulletin baudelairien*, ii no. 1, August 1966, and M. Eigeldinger, '"Le Thyrse", lecture thématique', in *Études baudelairiennes* viii, Neuchâtel, La Baconnière, 1976.
90. See Ch. II.
91. See ii. 644, and Ch. III n. 26.
92. See i. 1351 and Kopp, ed. cit., pp. 359–62 for details concerning the writing and the publication of the poem.

Chapter II

1. *Corr.* ii. 583.
2. ii. 496.
3. The first paragraph is particularly striking: it is quoted on p. 89 in Ch. III.

4. Alison Fairlie's criticism of some of Baudelaire's early and more conventional poems can also be applied to 'Un plaisant': 'the technique of first describing an object in detail or telling a story and then explaining the meaning rarely produces the best poetry. This frequent nineteenth-century device leaves us too conscious of the division between outer and inner worlds, and of the intrusion of an outside observer to explain and discuss.' (*Baudelaire: 'Les Fleurs du Mal'*, London, Ed. Arnold. 1960, p. 20.)

5. As in 'Les Petites Vieilles':

> — Avez-vous observé que maints cercueils de vieilles
> Sont presque aussi petits que celui d'un enfant?
> [. . .]
> Et lorsque j'entrevois un fantôme débile
> Traversant de Paris le fourmillant tableau,
> Il me semble toujours que cet être fragile
> S'en va tout doucement vers un nouveau berceau;

It has been suggested that in 'Le Désespoir de la vieille' there is a hidden reference to Rousseau's ninth 'Promenade'; but it would appear that 'Le Gâteau' is even more relevant. See Ch. III p. 76-7.

6. *A travers le XIXe siècle*, Paris, Minard, 1975, p. 351.

7. Ed. cit. p. 188.

8. See 'Le Crépuscule du soir', 'La Femme sauvage et la petite-maîtresse', 'Le Joujou du pauvre', and 'Les Yeux des pauvres' respectively.

9. A drawing by Gavarni from *Paris le soir* shows a fine lady accompanied by a gentleman softly touching two children sleeping on the street and bears the caption ' "Le plaisir rend l'âme si bonne" — Béranger'.

10. 'Les yeux du père disaient: "Que c'est beau! que c'est beau! on dirait que tout l'or du pauvre monde est venu se porter sur ces murs." — Les yeux du petit garçon: "Que c'est beau! que c'est beau! mais c'est une maison où peuvent seuls entrer les gens qui ne sont pas comme nous." — Quant aux yeux du plus petit, ils étaient trop fascinés pour exprimer autre chose qu'une joie stupide et profonde.' (i. 583.)

11. *Corr.*, ed. cit., ii. 238.

12. *Petits Poèmes en prose*, ed. Melvin Zimmerman, Manchester University Press, 1968, p. 114. The 'morale agréable' of *Morale du joujou* is apparent in the following passage: 'Cette facilité à contenter son imagination témoigne de la spiritualité de l'enfance dans ses conceptions artistiques. Le joujou est la première initiation de l'enfant à l'art, ou plutôt c'en est pour lui la première réalisation, et, l'âge mûr venu, les réalisations perfectionnées ne donneront pas à son esprit les mêmes chaleurs, ni les mêmes enthousiasmes, ni la même croyance.' (i. 583.)

13. 'Tous les mécréants de mélodrame, maudits, damnés, fatalement marqués d'un rictus qui court jusqu'aux oreilles, sont dans l'orthodoxie pure du rire.' (ii.531.)

14. See Benjamin Fondane, *Baudelaire et l'expérience du gouffre*, Paris, Seghers, 1947, p. 156.

15. Camille Pissarro, *Turpitudes sociales*, facsimile edition, Geneva, 1972. I am grateful to Christopher Lloyd for showing me a copy of this edition.
16. *Corr.* ii. 563. There has been much comment recently about Baudelaire's links with Proudhon. See in particular the bibliography under Oehler, Stenzel, and van Slyke.
17. 'Baudelaire between Marx, Sade and Satan', in *Baudelaire, Mallarmé, Valéry: New Essays in Honour of Lloyd Austin*, Cambrige University Press, 1982, p. 45.
18. Lois Boe Hyslop, 'Baudelaire, Proudhon, and "Le Reniement de saint Pierre"', *French Studies*, xxx. 3, p. 284: 'Like Proudhon, Baudelaire could only scorn those for whom "l'action n'est pas la sœur du rêve".'
19. i. 650.
20. See Ch. III p. 72 ff. for a fuller discussion.
21. i. 670.
22. Ed. cit., p. 146.
23. As in 'La Mort des pauvres', where death is described as 'le but de la vie'.
24. Op. cit., p. 155.
25. Notre mot éternel est-il: C'ÉTAIT ÉCRIT?
    — SUR LE LIVRE DE DIEU, dit l'Orient esclave;
    Et l'Occident répond: — SUR LE LIVRE DU CHRIST.
26. See Kopp, ed. cit., p. 203.
27. Malraux, *La Condition humaine*, Paris, Gallimard, 1946, p. 373.
28. B. Johnson, op. cit., pp. 83 ff.
29. Kopp, ed. cit., p. 337.
30. i. 650.
31. i. 661.
32. Ed. cit., p. 335.
33. ii. 455.
34. i. 546.
35. 'The Poetics of Irony in Baudelaire's *La Fanfarlo*', *Neophilologus*, lix, no. 2, Apr. 1975, pp. 165–89.
36. Cf. his remarks about Delacroix: 'Un autre trait de ressemblance avec Stendhal était sa propension aux formules simples, aux maximes brèves, pour la bonne conduite de la vie.' (ii. 758)
37. i. 668.
38. i. 673.
39. i. 672.
40. i. 671.
41. ii. 130.
42. i. 676.
43. i. 663.
44. i. 660.
45. i. 710.
46. i. 649.
47. i. 692.

48. i. 659. Cf. in the *Salon* of 1859: 'Pour moi, si j'étais invité à représenter l'Amour, il me semble que je le peindrais sous la forme d'un cheval enragé qui dévore son maître, ou bien d'un démon aux yeux cernés par la débauche et l'insomnie, traînant, comme un spectre ou un galérien, des chaînes bruyantes à ses chevilles, et secouant d'une main une fiole de poison, de l'autre le poignard sanglant du crime'. (ii. 639.)

49. *A la recherche du temps perdu*, 3 vols., Paris, Gallimard, 1954, i. 164.

50. Chateaubriand, *Œuvres romanesques et voyages*, 2 vols., Paris, Gallimard, 1969, i. 145.

51. Baudelaire's 'quotation', 'Presque tous nos malheurs nous viennent de n'avoir pas su rester dans notre chambre', is somewhat different from the original in Pascal: 'J'ai dit souvent que tout le malheur des hommes vient d'une seule chose, qui est de ne savoir pas demeurer en repos dans une chambre.' (*Pensées*, 136 Lafuma, 139 Brunschvicg.)

52. For an unequivocal allusion to Pascal see the tercets of 'Les Hiboux':

> Leur attitude au sage enseigne
> Qu'il faut en ce monde qu'il craigne
> Le tumulte et le mouvement;
>
> L'homme ivre d'une ombre qui passe
> Porte toujours le châtiment
> D'avoir voulu changer de place.

The straightforward moral message of 'Les Hiboux' contrasts strongly with the uncertainties of the prose poems. As Felix Leakey says, 'If one must have didacticism, one could scarcely wish for it in a more concise, engaging and assimilable form than this.' ('Baudelaire: The Poet as Moralist', in *Studies in Modern French Literature presented to P. Mansell Jones*, Manchester University Press, 1961, p. 200.)

53. Ed. cit. p. 291. For the passage in question see ii. 48-9.

54. 'Baudelaire and Emerson', *Romanic Review*, xxxiv, no. 3, Oct. 1943, p. 222.

55. i. 674.

56. Voltaire, *Lettres philosophiques*, xxv, Section III.

57. The difference is perhaps one of emphasis. Voltaire is aware of the distance between man and his world and other men, but he does not view it tragically. He is interested in action and in the way men can communicate with one another. He wants, no doubt, to diminish the distance, but he is not obsessed by the impossible task of suppressing it.

58. See 'Semper eadem'.

59. 'Les Fenêtres'.

60. It is possible that Baudelaire's use of the expresssion 'fusée' owes something to Poe's 'sky rocketing' (see Cl. Pichois's comments in i. 1472).

61. It was Laforgue who first drew attention to such comparisons as 'La nuit s'épaississait ainsi qu'une cloison' ('Le Balcon'). See my *Essai*

sur Laforgue et les 'Derniers Vers' suivi de Laforgue et Baudelaire,
Lexington, French Forum 1980, pp. 97, 98, 106. See also Ch. III p. 69.

62. André Breton, 'Premier Manifeste' in *Les Manifestes du Surréalisme*,
Paris, Eds. du Sagittaire, 1946, p. 47.
63. See Ch. III p. 88 note 67.
64. i. 670.
65. J.-P. Sartre, *Baudelaire*, Paris, Gallimard, 1947, pp. 185–6.
66. Luke 18: 11.
67. Ed. cit., p. 104.
68. G. Blin, *Le Sadisme de Baudelaire*, Paris, Corti, 1948, p. 86.
69. Her fantasy provides a startling contrast with that of the dandy Samuel
Cramer in *La Fanfarlo*, who to the natural charms of his mistress prefers
her theatrical costume: 'Je veux Colombine, rends-moi Colombine;
rends-la-moi telle qu'elle m'est apparue le soir qu'elle m'a rendu fou
avec son accoutrement fantasque et son corsage de saltimbanque!'
(i. 577.)
70. i. 668.

Chapter III

1. For example, 'A André Chénier' in *Les Contemplations* :

Oui, mon vers croit pouvoir, sans se mésallier,
Prendre à la prose un peu de son air familier.
André, c'est vrai; je ris quelquefois sur la lyre.
Voici pourquoi. Tout jeune encor, tâchant de lire
Dans le livre effrayant des forêts et des eaux,
J'habitais un parc sombre où jasaient des oiseaux,
Où des pleurs souriaient dans l'œil bleu des pervenches.

See also Gautier, *Poésies* (1830): 'Le Sentier', 'Rêve'.
2. In sending to Jean Morel an early version of 'Les Sept Vieillards'
Baudelaire writes: 'c'est le premier numéro d'une nouvelle série que je
veux tenter, et je crains bien d'avoir simplement réussi à dépasser les
limites assignées à la Poésie.' (*Corr.* i. 583.)
3. Paul Valéry, *Œuvres*, i, Paris, Gallimard, 1957, p. 1503.
4. i. 200. M. Ruff suggests that the poem was considerably longer,
covering the whole passage in *La Fanfarlo* ('Baudelaire et le poème en
prose', *Zeitschrift für französische Sprache und Literatur*, Jan. 1967,
p. 118).
5. In '*La Fanfarlo*' and '*Le Spleen de Paris*', London, Grant and Cutler,
1984, p. 15, Barbara Wright compares 'Le ruisseau, lit funèbre où s'en
vont les billets doux' (i. 574) with the original by Baudelaire or Prarond,
'Le ruisseau, lit funèbre où s'en vont les dégoûts'.
6. Kopp, ed. cit., p. xxxiv, is right to stress that in the three examples he
gives the prose comes after the verse: 'Elle n'est donc pas — comme trop
de critiques ont tendance à le croire — une première ébauche à partir

de laquelle se serait élaboré le poème en vers.' This would also be true of 'J'aime le souvenir . . . ', but possibly not of 'Harmonie du soir' and 'Mœsta et errabunda' which are also echoed in the passage, unless, of course, M. Ruff's hypothesis is correct, and the lost version covering the whole passage was an earlier version of these poems.

7. Quoted by Suzanne Bernard, op. cit., p. 442.

8. The reader might find it useful to have the whole of the first paragraph of Samuel's speech:

Quelle différence, et combien il reste peu du même homme, excepté le souvenir! mais le souvenir n'est qu'une souffrance nouvelle. Le beau temps que celui où le matin ne réveilla jamais nos genoux engourdis ou rompus par la fatigue des songes, où nos yeux clairs riaient à toute la nature, où notre âme ne raisonnait pas, mais où elle vivait et jouissait; où nos soupirs s'écoulaient doucement sans bruit et sans orgueil! que de fois, dans les loisirs de l'imagination, j'ai revu une de ces belles soirées automnales où les jeunes âmes font des progrès comparables à ces arbres qui poussent de plusieurs coudées par un coup de foudre. Alors je vois, je sens, j'entends; la lune réveille les gros papillons; le vent chaud ouvre les belles de nuit; l'eau des grands bassins s'endort. — Ecoutez en esprit les valses subites de ce piano mystérieux. Les parfums de l'orage entrent par les fenêtres; c'est l'heure où les jardins sont pleins de robes roses et blanches qui ne craignent pas de se mouiller. Les buissons complaisants accrochent les jupes fuyantes, les cheveux bruns et les boucles blondes se mêlent en tourbillonnant! — Vous souvient-il encore, Madame, des énormes meules de foin, si rapides à descendre, de la vieille nourrice si lente à vous poursuivre, et de la cloche si prompte à vous rappeler sous l'œil de votre tante, dans la grande salle à manger? (i. 560.)

9. i. 380 ff.

10. See 'Baudelaire ou la difficulté créatrice', in *Baudelaire: Études et témoignages*, Neuchâtel, La Baconnière, 1967, pp. 242–61.

11. See Ch. I, n. 3.

12. 'La prose ne doit pas être un mélange de vers' (Marmontel). 'Il faut éviter les vers dans la prose autant qu'il se peut, surtout les vers alexandrins' (Vaugelas). Quoted by Suzanne Bernard, op. cit., p. 35 n. 88.

13. Graham Chesters, 'The Transformation of a prose-poem: Baudelaire's "Crépuscule du soir" ', in *Baudelaire, Mallarmé, Valéry: New Essays in Honour of Lloyd Austin*, Cambridge University Press, 1982, pp. 24–37.

14. See my *Essai sur Laforgue et les 'Derniers Vers' suivi de Laforgue et Baudelaire*, Lexington, French Forum, 1980, p. 103, where Laforgue talks dismissively of the 'alexandrin à rimes plates, qui est bien la période du prédicateur'.

15. 'Manier savamment une langue, c'est pratiquer une espèce de sorcellerie évocatoire'. (ii. 118.) 'Qu'est-ce que l'art pur suivant la conception moderne? C'est créer une magie suggestive contenant à la fois l'objet et le sujet, le monde extérieur à l'artiste et l'artiste lui-même.' (ii. 598.)

16. Charlotte Schröer, *Les Petits Poèmes en prose von Baudelaire*, Leipzig, 1935; G. Streit, *Die Doppelmotive in Baudelaires 'Fleurs du Mal' und 'Petits Poèmes en prose'*, Zürich, Heits, 1929; J. B. Ratermanis, *Étude*

sur le style de Baudelaire d'après Les Fleurs du Mal et les Petits Poèmes en prose, Baden, Éds. Art et Science, 1949; *Les Fleurs du Mal*, edited by J. Crépet and G. Blin, Paris, Corti, 1942, pp. 335–7, 387–90; B. Johnson, op. cit., pp. 31–55, 103–60.

17. Op. cit., p. 141.
18. In 'Tintern Abbey'. See G. Bachelard, 'La Phénoménologie du rond' in *La Poétique de l'espace*, Paris, PUF, 1957, for a discussion of the notion of 'roundness'.
19. Op. cit., p. 53: 'La figure "manger des souvenirs" devient donc figure de la facticité de la figure poétique "boire le vin du souvenir" qu'elle littéralise et métonymise.'
20. See Ch. II n. 61.
21. Lautréamont, *Œuvres complètes*, Paris, Corti, 1963, p. 327.
22. See S. Freud, *Jokes and their Relation to the Unconscious*, Penguin, 1976, pp. 41–2.
23. See ii. 455: 'Les poètes, les artistes et toute la race humaine seraient bien malheureux, si l'idéal, cette absurdité, cette impossibilité était trouvé! Qu'est-ce que chacun ferait désormais de son pauvre *moi* — de sa ligne brisée?'
24. S. Bernard, op. cit., p. 119: 'Ces transformations dans le sens de la platitude trahissent ce que trahissent aussi beaucoup de poèmes de la dernière période: un essoufflement, un tarissement de l'imagination créatrice... une sorte d'enlisement aussi dans le prosaïsme que la conception même de son recueil condamnait Baudelaire à affronter sans cesse!'

The conclusion to the 1857 version read: 'Le rêve! le rêve! toujours le rêve maudit! — Il tue l'action et mange le temps! — Les rêves soulagent un moment la bête dévorante qui s'agite en nous. C'est un poison qui la soulage, mais qui la nourrit.

Où donc trouver une coupe assez profonde et un poignard assez épais pour noyer la Bête!'

The understatement of the final version can be compared in its effectiveness to that of 'La Corde'. See p. 101 note 33.
25. ii. 329–30.
26. 'La fantaisie est d'autant plus dangereuse qu'elle est plus facile et plus ouverte; dangereuse comme la poésie en prose, comme le roman, elle ressemble à l'amour qu'inspire une prostituée et qui tombe bien vite dans la puérilité ou dans la bassesse; dangereuse comme toute liberté absolue.' (ii. 644.)
27. For example, F. W. Leakey, *Baudelaire and Nature*, Manchester University Press, 1969, p. 79 and note 2.

The reader may find it helpful to have the first paragraph:

Supposons un bel espace de nature où tout verdoie, rougeoie, poudroie et chatoie en pleine liberté, où toutes choses, diversement colorées suivant leur constitution moléculaire, changées de seconde en seconde par le déplacement de l'ombre et de la lumière, et agitées par le travail intérieur du calorique, se trouvent en perpétuelle vibration, laquelle fait trembler les lignes et complète la loi du mouvement éternel et universel. — Une immensité, bleue quelquefois et verte souvent, s'étend jusqu'aux confins du ciel: c'est la mer. Les arbres sont verts, les gazons verts, les mousses vertes; le vert serpente dans les troncs, les tiges non mûres sont vertes; le vert est le fond de la nature, parce que le vert se marie facilement à tous les autres tons. Ce qui me frappe d'abord, c'est que partout, — coquelicots dans les gazons, pavots, perroquets, etc., — le rouge chante la gloire du vert; le noir, — quand il y en a, — zéro solitaire et insignifiant, intercède le secours du bleu ou du rouge. Le bleu, c'est-à-dire le ciel, est coupé de légers flocons blancs ou de masses grises qui trempent heureusement sa morne crudité, — et, comme la vapeur de la saison, — hiver ou été, — baigne, adoucit, ou engloutit les contours, la nature ressemble à un toton qui, mû par une vitesse accélérée, nous apparaît gris, bien qu'il résume en lui toutes les couleurs.

Likewise, Rosemary Lloyd sees Baudelaire's splendid piece on Marceline Desbordes-Valmore (II. 145–9) as 'a prose poem in its own right' (*Baudelaire's Literary Criticism*, Cambridge University Press, 1981, p. 191).

28. Flaubert, *Par les champs et par les grèves*, Paris, Conard, 1927, p. 295.
29. Op. cit. p. 118: 'Certes, les trois paragraphes qui terminent, à partir de 1864, *Le Crépuscule du Soir*, ne sont pas sans beauté, dans leur élan lyrique; mais lorsque Baudelaire les rajouta au texte primitif, purement anecdotique, conçu pour figurer dans le recueil *Fontainebleau*, comment n'a-t-il pas senti qu'il greffait un second poème sur le premier, différent de caractère et d'inspiration?'
30. ii. 596. Of Banville he writes: 'Le talent de Banville représente les belles heures de la vie' (ii. 164).
31. Rimbaud, *Œuvres*, Paris, Garnier, 1981, p. 351, Letter to Paul Demeny.
32. In *Derniers Vers* and *Jadis et naguère* respectively.
33. *Corr.* ii. 615.
34. The religious overtones come from the etymology of the word meaning 'God in us'.
35. i. 199.
36. 'Mœsta et errabunda', lines 21 and 25.
37. ii. 690.
38. As in 'La Femme sauvage et la petite-maîtresse', 'Les Yeux des pauvres', and 'Le Galant Tireur'.
39. Lemaître, ed. cit., p. 185.
40. Kopp, ed. cit., pp. 328–30; R. Jasinski, op. cit., pp. 359–62.
41. In 'La Maison du berger':

> Éva, qui donc es-tu? Sais-tu bien ta nature?
> Sais-tu quel est ici ton but et ton devoir?
> Sais-tu, que pour punir l'homme, sa créature,
> D'avoir porté la main sur l'arbre du savoir,
> Dieu permit qu'avant tout, de l'amour de soi-même
> En tout temps, à tout âge, il fît son bien suprême,
> Tourmenté de s'aimer, tourmenté de se voir?

Erasmus, *Praise of Folly*, provides another possible hidden intertext: 'For what is so foolish as to be pleased with yourself?' There is an illustration referring to this by Holbein, showing a fool in a mirror, reproduced in William Willeford, *The Fool and his Sceptre*, London, Ed. Arnold, 1969, p. 35.

The mirror in the prose poem contrasts with the one in the sonnet 'La Beauté':

Car j'ai, pour fasciner ces dociles amants,
De purs miroirs qui font toutes choses plus belles:
Mes yeux, mes larges yeux aux clartés éternelles!

Cf. also 'la foule se complaît dans les miroirs où elle se voit' (ii. 119–20).

42. i. 678.
43. i. 683
44. i. 365–74.
45. *'La Fanfarlo' and 'Le Spleen de Paris'*, by Barbara Wright and David H. T. Scott, London, Grant and Cutler, 1984, pp. 73–80.
46. See below, n. 54.
47. *Corr.* i. 676: 'Quel est donc l'imbécile (c'est peut-être un homme célèbre) qui traite si légèrement le Sonnet et n'en voit pas la beauté pythagorique?'
48. For example, 'Elle est vraiment laide; elle est fourmi, araignée, si vous voulez, squelette même; mais aussi elle est breuvage, magistère, sorcellerie! en somme, elle est exquise.'
49. Cf., for example, 'Harlem' by Bertrand:

Harlem, cette admirable bambochade qui résume l'école flamande, Harlem peint par Jean Breughel, Peeter Neefs, David Téniers et Paul Rembrandt.

Et le canal où l'eau bleue tremble, et l'église où le vitrage d'or flamboie, et le stoël où sèche le linge, au soleil, et les toits, verts de houblon.

Et les cigognes qui battent des ailes autour de l'horloge de la ville, tendant le col du haut des airs et recevant dans leur bec les gouttes de pluie.

Et l'insouciant bourgmestre qui caresse de la main son double menton, et l'amoureux fleuriste qui maigrit, l'œil attaché à une tulipe.

Et la bohémienne qui se pâme sur sa mandoline, et le vieillard qui joue du Rommelpot, et l'enfant qui enfle une vessie.

Et les buveurs qui fument dans l'estaminet borgne, et la servante de l'hôtellerie qui accroche à la fenêtre un faisan mort.

50. See Ch. I, p. 15 and note 47.
51. For example, 'Le Désespoir de la vieille', 'La Chambre double', 'Le Fou et la Vénus', 'Le Vieux Saltimbanque', 'Le Gâteau', 'Les Bienfaits de la lune'.
52. ii. 165.
53. Valéry, *Eupalinos, L'Âme et la danse, Dialogue de l'arbre*, Paris, Gallimard, 1944, p. 171.
54. J.-P. Sartre, *Situations II*, Paris, Gallimard, 1948, p. 88.

55. Max Jacob, unpublished letter quoted by Jean de Palacio in 'La Postérité du *Gaspard de la Nuit* : de Baudelaire à Max Jacob', *La Revue des lettres modernes*, nos. 336–9, 1973, 1, p. 161.
56. J. Cohen, *Structure du langage poétique*, Paris, Flammarion, 1977, pp. 69, 83, 92.
57. *Corr.* ii. 128, where he mentions '*Poèmes nocturnes* (essais de poésie lyrique en prose, dans le genre de *Gaspard de la Nuit*)'.
58. S. Bernard, op. cit., p. 403.
59. Letter from Huysmans to Mallarmé, Nov. 1882, quoted by Henri Mondor, *Vie de Mallarmé*, Paris, Gallimard, 1950, p. 421.
60. See in particular: Alphonse Rabbe, 'Le Centaure', 'Le Naufrage', 'L'Adolescence', in *Album d'un pessimiste*, ed. Jules Marsan, Paris, Les Presses françaises, 1924; Jules Lefèvre-Deumier, the section entitled 'Prose' in *Les Vespres de l'abbaye du val*, ed. G. Brunet, Paris, Les Presses françaises, 1924; Maurice de Guérin, 'Le Centaure' in *Œuvres complètes*, Paris, Sociéte Les Belles Lettres, 1947, tome I.
61. ii. 332.
62. *Corr.* i. 676.
63. ii. 329: 'Elle (i.e. la nouvelle) a sur le roman à vastes proportions cet immense avantage que sa brièveté ajoute à l'intensité de l'effet.'
64. S. Bernard, op. cit., p. 145.
65. Ibid., p. 112.
66. Huysmans, *A rebours*, Paris, Fasquelle, 1955, pp. 244–5.
67. ii. 579.
68. Cf. Flaubert, *Corr.*, ed. cit., iii. 322: 'Ce qui me semble, à moi, le plus haut dans l'Art (et le plus difficile), ce n'est ni de faire rire, ni de faire pleurer, ni de vous mettre en rut ou en fureur, mais d'agir à la façon de la nature, c'est-à-dire de *faire rêver*.'
69. 'Dans certains états de l'âme presque surnaturels, la profondeur de la vie se révèle tout entière dans le spectacle, si ordinaire qu'il soit, qu'on a sous les yeux. Il en devient le symbole.' (i. 659.) Cf. 'Il y a des moments de l'existence où le temps et l'étendue sont plus profonds, et le sentiment de l'existence immensément augmenté.' (i. 658.)
70. i. 392–4.
71. See 'Ce que dit la bouche d'ombre' in *Les Contemplations*.
72. Except, of course, in the anomalous final version of 'Le Crépuscule du soir'.
73. See 'Réponse à un acte d'accusation' in *Les Contemplations*.
74. See 'Portraits de maîtresses', which is clearly linked to 'La Femme sauvage et la petite-maîtresse'.
75. ii. 534.
76. See James Patty, 'Baudelaire and Bossuet on Laughter', *PMLA* Sept. 1965, pp. 459–61.
77. ii. 528.
78. H. Bergson, *Le Rire*.

79. ii. 530.
80. A. Breton, *Anthologie de l'humour noir*, Paris, Pauvert, 1966, p. 173: 'L'humour chez Baudelaire fait partie intégrante de sa conception du dandysme.'
81. ii. 712.
82. i. 661.
83. Michel Carrouges, *André Breton et les données fondamentales du Surréalisme*, Paris, Gallimard, 1950, p. 125.
84. ii. 539. Hogarth's caricature 'The Reward of Cruelty' which Baudelaire admired (see ibid., 565) readily fits the category of black humour.
85. ii. 535.
86. ii. 543.
87. ii. 549.
88. ii. 566
89. ii. 568-9.
90. Malraux, op. cit., p. 179.
91. L. Cellier, 'D'une rhétorique profonde: Baudelaire et l'oxymoron', in *Parcours initiatiques*, Neuchâtel, La Baconnière, 1977, p. 194.
92. Cf. 'Le dessin arabesque est le plus spiritualiste des dessins.' (i. 652.)
93. See Octavio Paz, *Children of the Mire*, Harvard University Press, 1974, p. vii.
94. Cf. also the figures in 'Les Dons des Fées', 'Les Tentations ou Éros, Plutus et la Gloire', and 'Le Joueur généreux'.

Chronology
of the publication of the prose poems

Round brackets indicate that a poem had already been published.

1855

Hommage à C. F. Denecourt, FONTAINEBLEAU, Paysages, Légendes, Souvenirs, Fantaisies, etc., Hachette, 1855

Le Crépuscule du soir   La Solitude

1857

Le Présent, 24 August, *Poëmes nocturnes* :
(Le Crépuscule du soir)   L'Horloge
(La Solitude)   La Chevelure
Les Projets   L'Invitation au voyage

1861

Revue fantaisiste, 1 November, *Poëmes en prose* :

I. (Le Crépuscule du soir)   VI. (L'Invitation au voyage)
II. (La Solitude)   VII. Les Foules
III. (Les Projets)   VIII. Les Veuves
IV. (L'Horloge)   IX. Le Vieux Saltimbanque
V. (La Chevelure)

1862

La Presse, 26 and 27 August, 24 September, *Petits poëmes en prose* : A Arsène Houssaye.

I. L'Étranger   XI. La Femme sauvage et la
II. Le Désespoir de la vieille   petite maîtresse
III. Le *Confiteor* de l'artiste   XII. (Les Foules)
IV. Un plaisant   XIII. (Les Veuves)
V. La Chambre double   XIV. (Le Vieux Saltimbanque)
VI. Chacun la sienne [Chacun   *
          sa chimère]   XV. Le Gâteau
VII. Le Fou et la Vénus   XVI. (L'Horloge)
VIII. Le Chien et le flacon   XVII. (Un hémisphère dans une
IX. Le Mauvais Vitrier   chevelure)
          *   XVIII. (L'Invitation au voyage)
                                   XIX. Le Joujou du pauvre
X. A une heure du matin   XX. Les Dons des fées

1863

Revue nationale et étrangère, 10 June, *Petits Poëmes en prose* :
Les Tentations ou Éros, Plutus et   La Belle Dorothée
            la gloire

Le Boulevard, 14 June, *Poëmes en prose* :
I. No title [Les Bienfaits de la   II. Laquelle est la vraie?
     lune]

Revue nationale et étrangère, 10 October, 10 December, *Petits Poëmes en prose* :
I. Une mort héroïque   Les Fenêtres
II. Le Désir de peindre   Déjà!

       *
Le Thyrse (A Franz Liszt)

1864

Figaro, 7 and 14 February, *Le Spleen de Paris*, *Poëmes en prose* :
La Corde (A Édouard Manet)   Enivrez-vous
(Le Crépuscule du soir)   *
Le Joueur généreux   Les Vocations
           Un cheval de race

La Vie Parisienne, 2 July and 13 August,
Les Yeux des pauvres
*
(Les Projets)

L'Artiste, 1 November, *Petits Poëmes en prose* :
(Une mort héroïque)   (La Corde)
La Fausse Monnaie

Revue de Paris, 25 December, *Le Spleen de Paris*, *Poëmes en prose* :
I. (Les Yeux des pauvres)   IV. Le Miroir
II. (Les Projets)   V. (La Solitude)
III. Le Port   VI. (La Fausse Monnaie)

1865

L'Indépendance belge, 21 June,
Les Bons Chiens (A. M. Joseph Stevens).

1866

Revue du XIXe siècle, 1 June, *Petits Poëmes lycanthropes* :
I. (La Fausse Monnaie)
II. (Le Diable) [Le Joueur généreux]

L'Événement, 12 June, *Le Spleen de Paris* :
(La Corde (A Édouard Manet))

La Petite Revue, 27 October,
(Les Bons Chiens) (A M. Joseph Stevens)

Le Grand Journal, 4 November,
(Les Bons Chiens)

1867

Revue nationale et étrangère, 31 August, 7, 14, 21, 28 September, 11 October
(Les Bons Chiens)   Portraits de maîtresses
            *   *
(L'Idéal et le Réel) [Laquelle est   'Any where out of the world'.
            la vraie?]   N'importe où hors du monde
            *   *
(Les Bienfaits de la Lune) [Dédié   Le Tir et le cimetière
            à Mlle B.]
            *

1869

Poems appearing for the first time in *Œuvres complètes*, Paris, Michel Lévy.
Le Galant Tireur   Mademoiselle Bistouri
La Soupe et les nuages   Assommons les pauvres!
Perte d'auréole

Select Bibliography

1 Editions of Le Spleen de Paris

J. Crépet, Petits Poëmes en prose (Le Spleen de Paris), Paris, Conard, 1926.

Daniel-Rops, Petits Poèmes en prose (Le Spleen de Paris), Paris, Les Belles Lettres, 1934.

H. Lemaître, Petits Poèmes en prose (Le Spleen de Paris), Paris, Garnier, 1962.

M. Ruff, Petits poèmes en prose (Le Spleen de Paris), Paris, Garnier-Flammarion, 1967.

M. Zimmerman, Petits Poèmes en prose, Manchester University Press, 1968.

R. Kopp, Petits Poëmes en prose, Paris, Corti, 1969.

Cl. Pichois, Le Spleen de Paris in Œuvres complètes, i. Paris, Gallimard, 1975.

M. Milner, Le Spleen de Paris: Petits Poèmes en prose, Paris, Imprimerie nationale, 1979.

2 General works and studies relating wholly or in part to Baudelaire and Le Spleen de Paris

BENJAMIN, Walter, Charles Baudelaire: A Lyric Poet in the Era of High Capitalism, London, NLB, 1973.

BERNARD, Suzanne, Le Poème en prose de Baudelaire jusqu'à nos jours, Paris, Nizet, 1959.

BERSANI, Leo, Baudelaire and Freud, Berkeley, University of California Press, 1977.

BLIN, Georges, Le Sadisme de Baudelaire, Paris, Corti, 1948.

BORNEQUE, Jacques-Henry, 'Les Poèmes en prose de Baudelaire', L'Information littéraire, no. 5, 1953, pp. 177–82.

Catalogue de l'exposition Baudelaire, Bibliothèque Nationale, 1957.

CELLIER, Léon, 'D'une rhétorique profonde: Baudelaire et l'oxymoron', in Parcours initiatiques, Neuchâtel, La Baconnière, 1977.

CHAMBERS, Ross, 'The Artist as Performing Dog', Comparative Literature, xxiii, Fall, 1971, pp. 312–24.

—— ' "L'art sublime du comédien" ou le regardant et le regardé', Saggi e ricerche di letteratura francese, xi, 1971, pp. 189–260.

—— ' "Frôler ceux qui rôdent": le paradoxe du saltimbanque', Revue des sciences humaines, xlii, no. 167, 1977, pp. 347–63.

117

CHÉREL, Albert, *La Prose poétique française*, Paris, L'Artisan du livre, 1940.

CHESTERS, Graham, 'The Transformation of a Prose-Poem: Baudelaire's "Crépuscule du soir" ', in *Baudelaire, Mallarmé, Valéry: New Essays in Honour of Lloyd Austin*, Cambridge University Press, 1982.

CITRON, Pierre, *La Poésie de Paris dans la littérature française de Rousseau à Baudelaire*, 2 vols., Paris, Éds de Minuit, 1961.

COHEN, Jean, *Structure du langage poétique*, Paris, Flammarion, 1977.

—— *Le Haut Langage*, Paris, Flammarion, 1979.

DANIEL-ROPS, 'Baudelaire, poète en prose', *La Grande Revue*, no. 136, 1931, pp. 534–55.

DROST, Wolfgang, 'Baudelaire between Marx, Sade, and Satan', in *Baudelaire, Mallarmé, Valéry: New Essays in Honour of Lloyd Austin*, Cambridge University Press, 1982.

EIGELDINGER, Marc, 'A propos de l'image du thyrse', *Revue d'histoire littéraire de la France*, no. 75, 1975, pp. 110–12.

—— 'Le *Thyrse*, lecture thématique', in *Études baudelairiennes*, viii, Neuchâtel, La Baconnière, 1976.

FAIRLIE, Alison, *Baudelaire: 'Les Fleurs du Mal'*, London, Edward Arnold, 1960.

—— 'Observations sur les *Petits poèmes en prose*' and 'Quelques remarques sur les *Petits poèmes en prose*', in *Imagination and Language: Collected essays on Constant, Baudelaire, Nerval, and Flaubert*, Cambridge University Press, 1981.

FONDANE, Benjamin, *Baudelaire et l'expérience du gouffre*, Paris, Seghers, 1947.

FÜGLISTER, Robert L., 'Baudelaire et le thème des bohémiens', in *Études baudelairiennes*, ii, Neuchâtel, La Baconnière, 1971.

GALAND, René, *Baudelaire: poétiques et poésie*, Paris, Nizet, 1969.

GILMAN, Margaret, 'Baudelaire and Emerson', *Romanic Review*, xxxiv, no. 3, Oct. 1943, pp. 211–22.

GUIETTE, Robert, 'Vers et prose chez Baudelaire', in *Journées Baudelaire*, Actes du colloque Namur — Bruxelles, 10–13 Oct. 1967, Brussels, 1968, pp. 36–46.

—— 'Des "Paradis artificiels" aux "Petits Poëmes en prose" ', in *Études baudelairiennes*, iii, Neuchâtel, La Baconnière, 1973.

HIDDLESTON, J. A., *Essai sur Laforgue et les 'Derniers Vers' suivi de Laforgue et Baudelaire*, Lexington, French Forum, 1980.

—— 'Baudelaire and the Poetry of Prose', *Nineteenth-Century French Studies*, xii, nos. 1 & 2, Fall–Winter, 1983-4, pp. 124–37.

—— 'Baudelaire, Manet, et "La Corde" ', *Bulletin baudelairien*, xix, no. 1, 1984, pp. 7–11.

—— ' "Fusée", Maxim, and Commonplace in Baudelaire', *Modern Language Review*, lxxx, no. 3, July 1985, pp. 563–70.

HYSLOP, Lois Boe, 'Baudelaire, Proudhon, and "Le Reniement de saint Pierre" ', *French Studies*, xxx, 3, pp. 273–86.

JASINKSKI, René, *A travers le XIXe siècle*, Paris, Minard, 1975.

JOHNSON, Barbara, 'Quelques conséquences de la différence anatomique des textes: pour une théorie du poème en prose', *Poétique*, xxviii, 1976, pp. 450–65.

— *Défigurations du langage poétique*, Paris, Flammarion, 1979.

JONES, Louisa E., *Sad Clowns and Pale Pierrots: Literature and the Popular Comic Arts in 19th-Century France*, Lexington, French Forum, 1984.

JOUVE, Pierre Jean, '*Le Spleen de Paris*', *Mercure de France*, cccxxii, Sept. 1954, pp. 32–9.

KLEIN, Richard, ' "Bénédiction" | "Perte d'auréole": Parables of Interpretation', *Modern Language Notes*, lxxxv, no. 4, May 1970, pp. 515–28.

LEAKEY, F. W., 'Baudelaire: The Poet as Moralist', in *Studies in Modern French Literature presented to P. Mansell Jones*, Manchester University Press, 1961.

— 'Les Esthétiques de Baudelaire: le "système" des années 1844–47', *Revue des sciences humaines*, cxxvii, July–Sept. 1967, pp. 481–96.

LEBOIS, André, *Prestiges et actualité des 'Petits Poèmes en prose'*, *Archives des lettres modernes*, no. 18, 1958.

MAURON, Ch., *Le Dernier Baudelaire*, Paris, Corti, 1966.

NIES, Fritz, *Poesie in prosaischer Welt: Untersuchungen zum Prosagedicht bei Aloysius Bertrand und Baudelaire*, Heidelberg, Carl Winter, 1964.

OEHLER, Dolf, 'Le Caractère double de l'héroïsme et du beau modernes', in *Études baudelairiennes*, viii, Neuchâtel, La Baconnière, 1976.

PAZ, Octavio, *Children of the Mire: Modern Poetry from Romanticism to the Avant-Garde*, Harvard University Press, 1974.

PICHOIS, Cl., 'Baudelaire ou la difficulté créatrice', in *Baudelaire: études et témoignages*, Neuchâtel, La Baconnière, 1967.

— 'Baudelaire devant la sociocritique ouest-allemande', in *Études baudelairiennes*, ix, Neuchâtel, La Baconnière, 1981.

PIZZORUSSO, Arnaldo, ' "Le Mauvais Vitrier" ou l'impulsion inconnue', in *Études baudelairiennes*, viii, Neuchâtel, La Baconnière, 1976.

PRÉVOST, Jean, *Baudelaire: essai sur l'inspiration et la création poétiques*, Paris, Mercure de France, 1953.

RATERMANIS, J. B., *Étude sur le style de Baudelaire*, Baden, Éds Art et Science, 1949.

RAUHUT, Franz, *Das französische Prosagedicht*, Hamburg, Friedrichsen und de Gruyter, 1929.

REBEYROL, Ph., 'Baudelaire et Manet', *Les Temps modernes*, xlviii, Oct. 1949, pp. 707–25.

RUFF, M. A., *Baudelaire*, Paris, Hatier, 1966.

— 'Baudelaire et le poème en prose', *Zeitschrift für französische Sprache und Literatur*, lxxvii, Jan. 1967, pp. 116–23.

SARTRE, J.-P., *Baudelaire*, Paris, Gallimard, 1947.

SCHRÖER, Charlotte, *'Les Petits Poèmes en prose' von Baudelaire, eine Gedankendichtung, als Zeit- und Charakterdokument*, University of Jena dissertation, Leipzig, 1935.

SLYKE, Gretchen van, 'Dans l'intertexte de Baudelaire et de Proudhon: pourquoi faut-il assommer les pauvres?', *Romantisme*, no. 45, 1984, pp. 57–77.

STAROBINSKI, Jean, 'Sur quelques répondants allégoriques du poète', *Revue d'histoire littéraire de la France*, lxvii, Apr.–June 1967, pp. 402–12.

—— *Portrait de l'artiste en saltimbanque*, Geneva, Skira, 1970.

STENZEL, Hartmut, 'Quelques souvenirs socialistes dans l'œuvre de Baudelaire', *Bulletin baudelairien*, xii, no. 1, 1976, pp. 3–13.

STREIT, Gertrud, *Die Doppelmotive in Baudelaires 'Fleurs du Mal' und 'Petits Poèmes en prose'*, Zürich, Heits, 1929.

WELSFORD, Enid, *The Fool: His Social and Literary History*, London, Faber, 1935.

WING, Nathaniel, 'The Poetics of Irony in Baudelaire's *La Fanfarlo*', *Neophilologus*, lix, no. 2, April 1975, pp. 165–89.

WOHLFARTH, Irving, ' "Perte d'Auréole": The Emergence of the Dandy', *Modern Language Notes*, lxxxv, 1970, pp. 529–71.

WRIGHT, Barbara, and SCOTT, D. H. T., *'La Fanfarlo' and 'Le Spleen de Paris'*, London, Grant and Cutler, 1984.

ZIMMERMAN, Melvin, 'La Genèse du symbole du thyrse chez Baudelaire', *Bulletin baudelairien*, ii, no. 1, 1966, pp. 8–11.

Index

121